God's Plan Man's Need Our Mission

by G. Christian Weiss

Director of Missions
Back to the Bible Broadcast

75¢

order from

Back to the Bible Broadcast

Box 82808   Lincoln, Nebraska 68501

85,000 printed to date—1971
(5-0761—85M—91)

Printed in the United States of America

Foreword

Even though only 5 percent of the world's population lives in a stone-age culture, the general concept of missions seems to have taken on a stone-age image. One mission executive has said it is easier to get five candidates to go to the stone-agers of West Irian than to get one candidate to go to the teenagers of Tokyo.

But the real issue of missions is far broader than either stone-agers or teenagers—it is to confront every person with the gospel and to give him an opportunity to make a knowledgeable decision to accept or reject Jesus Christ.

God's Plan, Man's Need, Our Mission sets forth a scriptural world view of missions. It shows the imperativeness of really knowing what God's program is, the urgency of our having a new consciousness and a new conviction of man's need, and the importance of realizing that Christ has sent us into the world even as the Father sent Him into the world.

G. Christian Weiss is well qualified to write about missions. After graduating from a Bible institute and seminary, he pastored a church for three years and then went to Morocco as a missionary under the Gospel Missionary Union. After a term on the field, Dr. Weiss was appointed the president of the Gospel Missionary Union at the age of 30—probably being the youngest person ever to serve as president of a foreign mission society. Dr. Weiss served in that capacity for 12 years and then, after having prayed about the decision for three years, left that position to become director of the Back to the Bible Missionary Agency. At the Back to the Bible Broadcast he has been known as the "Voice of Foreign Missions."

Dr. Weiss not only has a grasp of the world missionary situation as a missions executive, but he has also personally visited every continent. His firsthand contact with the field—which is the world—makes this an important book, for it is the outgrowth of knowledge, experience and compassion.

The cause of missions has permeated every area of Dr. Weiss's life. He has effectively communicated his vision to his children, and two of them now serve as foreign missionaries.

May this book give you insight into God's missionary program and help you to understand the significance of Christ's words when He said, "As my Father hath sent me, even so send I you" (John 20:21).

—Harold J. Berry
Literature Editor

Contents

Chapter   **Page**

Part 1

1. A Clear Comprehension of God's Plan . 9
2. The Nature of God's Plan 14
3. The Unchangeableness of God's Plan . . 24
4. The Present Part of God's Plan . . . 30
5. A New Consciousness of God's Power . . 37
6. A New Conviction of Man's Need . . 49
7. A New Compulsion of Divine Love . . 56
8. A New Confrontation With Opportunities 67
9. A New Criterion of Values 75

Part 2

10. God's Stock Market 85
11. Loaves and Fish 94

12. Boats and Nets 100

13. A Man Who Surrendered His Son . . 105

Part 3

14. Like Mandate 113

15. Like Manner 118

16. Like Mission 129

17. Like Message 141

18. Like Motive 150

19. Like Mantle 164

Part 1

What Is Needed Among Christians Today?

Chapter 1

A Clear Comprehension
of God's Plan

What is needed among God's people in this generation?

There is failure and impotence in the Christian church. Religious and secular spokesmen alike point out its apparent sickness and ineffectiveness. Many people are prescribing various "cures," but many of these widely miss the mark. Some would only contribute to further weakness.

We need an answer to the question, What is needed to meet these deficiencies in the church? I think the *true* remedies can be prescribed only from the sole authoritative guidebook, the Bible.

In the field of medicine there are authoritative reference books to which medical doctors may turn for information and guidance. Churches today have tended to go to the wrong reference books for help and spiritual guidance. They have listened too long to the words and voices of men. They have applied remedies prescribed by human genius, and I fear they have missed the wisdom available through the divine guide, the Book of God. Neglect of the Word of God produces Christians who are susceptible to defeats and spiritual diseases.

In the light of the Book, what is needed among Christians today?

First, we certainly need *a clear comprehension of God's plan for the world*. This is God's world. He made it. It did not just appear without a cause by some process of natural laws. The most credible thing to believe about the existence of this world is what the Bible says: The world was created by an eternal, self-existent, all-powerful, intelligent God.

"In the beginning God created the heaven and the earth" (Gen. 1:1). This is the opening statement of the Bible. God created. What could be more satisfying or intelligent? It is simple yet sublime. God created everything that is in the world, and to crown all the rest of His creative work, He made man. This same fact is repeated in the New Testament: "All things were made by him; and without him was not any thing made that was made" (John 1:3).

Because it is God's world, He also sustains it. Paul said concerning Jesus Christ, God's Son, "All things were created by him, and for him: . . . and by him all things consist" (Col. 1:16,17). "Consist" here means "hold together." We are also told that he upholds "all things by the word of His power" (Heb. 1:3). It is God alone who sustains the world. He keeps the stars and planets in their precise places. He keeps our hearts beating and our lungs breathing, giving us life and breath and health. "In Him we live, and move, and have our being" (Acts 17:28).

Besides creating and sustaining the world, God is in control of it. Things have not been wrested out of His control, nor has He forsaken His creation through grief, disappointment or offense. God has neither been defeated in His own universe nor thwarted in His own creation.

Many people throughout the world are worried. Some Christians wring their hands in despair and ask, "What is this world coming to?" But our God is not worried nor bewildered by the things that are happening in today's world.

This is God's world, and He has a plan for it. The Bible is clear about this. Speaking of Christ, Ephesians 1:11 says, "In whom also we have obtained an inheritance, being predestinated according to the purpose of him who worketh all things after the counsel of his own will." This asserts that God causes all things to advance in keeping with His own will and plan, and nothing ever has or ever can thwart His purpose, which is integrally built into this plan.

In the third chapter of Ephesians there is an expression that is similar to the one in chapter 1: "According to the eternal purpose which he purposed in Christ Jesus our Lord" (v. 11). Here we are assured not only that God has a plan and purpose for the world, but also that this plan is an eternal purpose, which He planned in and through Jesus Christ, His Son. God's plan is eternal, existing before the creation of man and even before the creation of the world.

The Prophet Isaiah, speaking about a revealed purpose of God for his day, said, "The Lord of hosts hath sworn, saying, Surely as I have thought, so shall it come to pass; and as I have purposed [planned], so shall it stand. . . . This is the purpose that is purposed upon the whole earth: and this is

11

the hand that is stretched out upon all the nations. For the Lord of hosts hath purposed, and who shall disannul it? And His hand is stretched out, and who shall turn it back?" (Isa. 14:24,26,27). Speaking through the same prophet, God also said, "I have spoken it, I will also bring it to pass; I have purposed it, I will also do it" (46:11).

This great earth, with its billions of human beings, is not at the mercy of blind fate or blind force. It is in the hands of God. He made it, He sustains it, He controls it, and He has an eternal plan devised for it and for its people.

Not only does God have a plan for His world, but He is also working out that plan. God is carrying out His purpose in the world. In Ephesians 3:11 we are assured that He works all things according to His own plan and purpose. When Jesus Christ was here on the earth, He made the assertion, "My Father worketh hitherto, and I work" (John 5:17). His adversaries had found fault with Him for healing a man on the Sabbath Day, arguing that no work ought to be done on the Sabbath. In effect He said, "God, My Father, has always been at work in the world. He has been working out His plan and purpose. He has never ceased working. He never rests. And I am at work with Him in His purpose. Therefore, I do not cease nor grow weary nor rest."

Often in the four Gospels the expression occurs, "that the scripture might be fulfilled." Over and over again in the life of Jesus Christ the Spirit affirms, "that it might be fulfilled which was spoken" (Matt. 2:15). God had revealed a wonderful plan in the Holy Scriptures, and during

12

the lifetime of Jesus Christ on earth He was in the process of fulfilling that plan and purpose.

But certain men hated Jesus. They were determined to oppose Him, to reject Him, and even to do away with Him. Ultimately they saw to it that He was crucified. But by this they did not either thwart the purpose of God or counteract His eternal plan. Through all the things that happened to Jesus—during His life and in His death—God was working out His eternal plan and purpose.

God's plan for the world cannot be defeated. It cannot be thwarted. It cannot be annulled. This is a foundational assurance.

Chapter 2

The Nature of God's Plan

Since God has a plan which He is carrying out for this world, it is normal for us to ask, Just what is God's plan? What is God doing in the world? What does He desire to achieve?

We could never detect His plan merely by looking at the world as such. Not even by looking back over history can we specifically delineate it, although history does yield evidences of some things God has been doing in the world.

Certainly not in this present pattern of scenes in our world today can we, of ourselves, detect the divine plan. The world is so complicated, so bewildering, so fraught with complexities and perplexities, and so filled with troubles that it is extremely difficult—if not impossible—to trace the working of God's plan. This may be the reason many Christians are confused and mystified. They are trying to discover God's plan among the complexities of contemporary life, and it has left them reeling and protesting, We can't figure out what God is doing.

We are seeing only the underside of the loom, the "wrong" side of God's handiwork, not the "pattern" side. Someday we will see the top side and then all will be clear. But until that day comes, we must trust in God's Word and the Spirit's illumination in order to comprehend the nature of the divine plan and purpose for men and for the world. Only from God's Book can we determine God's plan. The Bible is primarily a Book of divine revelation.

The Divine Revelation

Many Christians seem to regard the Bible as merely a book of "recipes" to cheer them when they are discouraged, to comfort them when they are sad, to give them a lift when they have failed and feel blue, or to raise their spirits when they have sustained losses. They routinely go to favorite passages in the Bible to find recipes for these various situations. The Bible does have recipes for our needs and hurts, but this great Book is far more than a book of personal recipes for our petty personal hurts and grievances. The Bible is not primarily a book of recipes; it is primarily a Book of revelation. It reveals God. It reveals the nature of God, the Person of God and the attributes of God. It reveals His wisdom, His mercy, His greatness and His love.

Not only does the Bible reveal the Person of God, it also discloses His divine plan. It shows us God's design for the world and for humanity. By so doing, it reveals the nature of man. This Book demonstrates the fact that men are sinners, that they are born with sinful, depraved natures, and that they have a tendency toward that which is sinful and evil. Therefore, they are desperately in need of a divine work of inward regeneration, a

15

work which only God can achieve in human nature.

The plan of God revealed in the Bible is His plan to bring glory to Himself, and the redemption of humanity is one of the chief ways He does this. The plan of redemption asserts that without God men are hopeless sinners. They have committed acts of sin against the laws of God and against their own moral consciences. As a result of these sins and apart from salvation, mankind is doomed by divine justice to eternal condemnation and irremediable separation from God Himself. The plan of redemption reveals that men cannot save themselves. They need outside help. They need a Saviour. The Bible also reveals God's glorious plan for providing a Saviour for men and tells us that this Saviour is Jesus Christ, God's own eternal Son.

The Biblical Key

Exactly what is included in God's plan for man? What does it demand? In Luke 24:45-49 we find what I believe to be the key passage of the entire Bible. Luke 24 is a record of the events which occurred after Jesus' death and resurrection. When Christ was crucified on Calvary's cross, His disciples were thrown into utter chaos and confusion simply because they had not understood what God's plan was. They had not comprehended what was written in the Scriptures. They had been convinced and had believed that this Man, Jesus, had come into the world from heaven to be the Messiah. They believed that He was the Son of God and that, in some way, He would become the Saviour of men. But they did not understand just how this would be achieved, nor did they grasp what He came to do at that time. Though they believed He came to be the Saviour, they did not know how He would save the world. In their misconception, they apparently thought He would set up a kingdom of righteousness on earth then and there and that gradually His kingdom would spread and prevail over the earth until all men would become children of God. Hence, when He was arrested, crucified, and buried, all their hopes and dreams collapsed, and they were thrown into confusion.

Having previously failed to understand these things, they were filled with perplexity and doubt. They had believed that Jesus was the Son of God and that He was the Messiah. In this belief they had left all and followed Him. But when they saw Him crucified on Golgotha's hill, they were thrown into mental and spiritual chaos. Then Jesus appeared to them and showed them from the Scriptures that this was the very thing that was written of Him—that God's plan of redemption for mankind required that He suffer and die on a cross for the sins of the world.

"Then opened he their understanding, that they might understand the scriptures, and said unto them, Thus it is written, and thus it behoved Christ to suffer, and to rise from the dead the third day: and that repentance and remission of sins should be preached in his name among all nations, beginning at Jerusalem. And ye are witnesses of these things. And, behold, I send the promise of my Father upon you: but tarry ye in the city of Jerusalem, until ye be endued with power from on high" (Luke 24:45-49).

Christ's Death for Mankind Essential

This is one major part of the divine plan of redemption: that God's only begotten Son, Jesus Christ, must suffer and die for the sins of the world. We can never truly understand the Scriptures until we understand them in the light of this great truth and understand that this was a vital part of God's eternal plan. "It behoved Christ to suffer, and to rise from the dead" (24:46). The atoning death of Jesus Christ was an essential part of the plan of God, even though His disciples had not previously seen nor comprehended it. Now He "opened . . . their understanding" (v. 45), and they comprehended it. As a result of this comprehension, they spent the rest of their lives preaching "Jesus Christ, and him crucified" (I Cor. 2:2).

World Evangelization Also Essential

Jesus pointed out to His disciples another vital part of the divine plan: "That repentance and remission of sins should be preached in his name among all nations" (Luke 24:47).

These are the two fundamental parts of God's great plan—the atoning death of Christ on Calvary's cross and the evangelization of the world by the Church. The plan demanded that God's Son, Jesus Christ, come into this world incarnate and die as a Man on the cross for the sins of mankind. This having been accomplished, the entire world must be apprised of what He has done. Beginning at Jerusalem on the Day of Pentecost, His followers, who comprised the newly founded Church, must

18

begin proclaiming the Good News to men everywhere—in Jerusalem, in Judea and Samaria and unto the uttermost part of the earth (Acts 1:8).

Actually, there are three major parts to God's divine plan: the atoning death of Christ, the evangelization of the world, and finally, the return of Jesus to the earth. This is the ultimate phase. Jesus Christ will come again from heaven and will gather out of this world all those who have been redeemed by faith in Him through the preaching of the gospel—from every kindred, tongue, people and nation.

These aspects of the plan of God are repeatedly emphasized in the Scriptures. The Apostle Paul wrote, for example: "God was in Christ, reconciling the world unto himself, not imputing their trespasses unto them; and hath committed unto us the word of reconciliation. . . . We pray you in Christ's stead, be ye reconciled to God" (II Cor. 5:19,20).

Paul declared that Christ "gave himself a ransom for all, to be testified in due time" (I Tim. 2:6). He gave Himself a ransom for the sins of all men on Calvary's cross "in due time" (at the proper time). His redeeming work, the ransom price, must be proclaimed to the world. Repentance and remission of sins must be preached to all men in His name. When this has been accomplished and the Church completed, He will come again to receive to Himself all who have believed unto salvation.

19

The Three Divine Interventions

It is apparent that the plan of redemption called for some major, dramatic, divine interventions, or "interruptions," in human history. The first such interruption occurred when the Son of God came to this earth. The Bible says, "When the fulness of time was come, God sent forth his Son, made of a woman, made under the law" (Gal. 4:4). This we call the intervention of divine incarnation.

Paul described this intervention as the "great . . . mystery of godliness" (I Tim. 3:16). Redemption required and demanded this. The night Jesus was born in Bethlehem, the angels from heaven announced, "Unto you is born this day in the city of David a Saviour, which is Christ the Lord" (Luke 2:11). The angels described this as "good tidings of great joy" (v. 10).

The Apostle Paul expressed it: "This is a faithful saying, and worthy of all acceptation, that Christ Jesus came into the world to save sinners" (I Tim. 1:15). This was the first of three great divine interventions in human history—the Son of God came to earth and became the "Son of man" (Luke 19:10).

The second great intervention was the coming of the Spirit of God on the Day of Pentecost. Jesus, in His incarnation, took upon Himself the form of man in order that He might make atonement for the sins of the world. But the Holy Spirit came into the world on the Day of Pentecost to take up His abode in the members of the Body of Christ, the Church, making them His own temple. He came on the Day of Pentecost to fulfill the second great part of God's plan, the evangelization of the whole world. Jesus came to fulfill that part of the plan which He alone could fulfill—suffering, dying and rising from the dead the third day. The Holy Spirit came in order that believers might be empowered to carry out their part—bearing Christ's witness to the ends of the earth.

According to the first chapter of the Book of Acts, the disciples were with Jesus just prior to His ascension and return to heaven. They raised the question that was so firmly fixed in their minds: "Lord, wilt thou at this time restore again the kingdom to Israel?" (v. 6). He responded by saying, "It is not for you to know the times or the seasons, which the Father hath put in His own power. But ye shall receive power, after that the Holy Ghost is come upon you: and ye shall be witnesses unto me both in Jerusalem, and in all Judaea, and in Samaria, and unto the uttermost part of the earth" (vv. 7,8). Then, on the Day of Pentecost, when they were gathered together in Jerusalem in one place, there suddenly came a sound, as of a mighty, rushing wind. The Holy Spirit descended from heaven to take up His fixed dwelling place in those men and to fill them with power to proclaim the gospel to the world.

The Holy Spirit is still here. He still indwells believers. He still resides in the Church on earth, which is Christ's Body and the Spirit's temple. His primary purpose on the earth at this time is to dwell within the Church and empower it to fulfill the second major part of God's divine plan—the carrying of the witness of the gospel of Jesus Christ to the uttermost part of the earth.

These two great divine interventions were for the purpose of providing for men a way of repentance and remission of sins.

According to the Scriptures, there will also be a third intervention of God in human events. The heavens will one day open, and a divine Person will return to this world's stage—Jesus Christ, the sovereign Son of God. The One who was here 2000 years ago and who died on the cross to make atonement for the sins of men, the One who commanded His disciples, under the power of the Holy Spirit, to go into all the world and proclaim His gospel to every creature—He will come again! And when He comes, He will gather His own redeemed ones out of "all nations, and kindreds, and people, and tongues" (Rev. 7:9).

The Bible describes this glorious coming event vividly: "Behold, he cometh with clouds; and every eye shall see him" (Rev. 1:7). "This same Jesus . . . shall so come in like manner as ye have seen him go into heaven" (Acts 1:11). "The Lord Jesus shall be revealed from heaven with his mighty angels" (II Thess. 1:7). "Then shall all the tribes of the earth mourn, and they shall see the Son of man coming in the clouds of heaven with power and great glory" (Matt. 24:30). "The glorious appearing of our great God and our Saviour Jesus Christ" (Titus 2:13). Statements and promises concerning the coming of Christ are numerous in the Scriptures, in both the Old and the New Testaments.

This is God's plan—His divine scheme for the redemption of men. His only begotten Son had to come into the world and die to make atonement for our sins. The Church must preach throughout all the world repentance and remission of sins through faith in Him. Then Jesus will come again to gather His own redeemed ones out of all the nations of the earth and will later establish His glorious kingdom of righteousness upon this earth. This will be the glorious climax to it all.

This is what we as Christians must understand. And if we understand these things as the plan of God, we will know what we are to do now in this dispensation—preach the message of Christ to all men everywhere. Seeing these things taking place, we will remain calm and composed, regardless of the many distressing things that are going on among the nations of the earth in our day and generation. Clarity of spiritual understanding will lead to calmness of spirit and to confident faith.

Chapter 3

The Unchangeableness of God's Plan

It has been emphasized that unless we understand the nature of God's plan and purpose in the world, we may become discouraged and bewildered by the things that are taking place around us.

In summary, God does have a plan, revealed in the Scriptures, and He is working out that plan. It involves three divine interventions in the history of man. The first was the incarnation of the Son of God to become man's Redeemer by making atonement for human sin through His own substitutionary death on the cross. The second was the coming of the Holy Spirit to the Church on the Day of Pentecost to enable it to carry out the next vital part of His plan, the evangelization of the world. The third great act in the drama of redemption will be the Second Coming of Jesus Christ to this earth to gather to Himself all those who have believed the gospel and who, through the new birth, have become children of God, both the living and the dead. Following this, God will establish His own kingdom of righteousness on the earth.

His Plan Embraces the Whole World

There is one special emphasis about the plan of God as revealed in the Bible that must be stressed: His plan of salvation, the reconciling of sinners to Himself, embraces the whole world. This has already been implied, but at this point I want to underscore the universal nature of God's provision of salvation. This is an aspect of the divine plan of which we as Christians need to be keenly aware in our day, but it is one which we often forget or omit. God's redemptive plan embraces the whole world—every nation, race, family and tribe—every son of Adam. This is the constant and consistent emphasis of the Scriptures.

In the first eleven chapters of the Book of Genesis, God is seen dealing with the human family as a single unit. There are no races and no distinctions. There is just one human family, and God is seen manifesting His interest in that family and His love for it. When the human race, in its comparatively early history, corrupted itself by rebellion and iniquity, so that "every imagination of the thoughts of [man's] heart was only evil continually" (6:5), God destroyed mankind with a great flood. He then gave the world a new start with a righteous man as its head. But again the race rebelled, departing from God and corrupting itself. So in Genesis 12 we see God doing a new thing in the earth, and from that point onward, throughout the rest of the Old Testament, we see Him following a new course.

God called Abraham to separate himself from his own country and kindred and go to another land that would be given to him and to his posterity. The children of Abraham were God's Chosen People. Throughout the Old Testament the story unfolds concerning God's dealings with these Chosen People, the descendants of Abraham, the nation of Israel.

The Divine Purpose in the Chosen People

This aspect of God's working has often been misunderstood and misconstrued. The children of Israel themselves misinterpreted God's purpose in calling them to be His Chosen People. They assumed that God was concerned primarily, if not exclusively, with *them* in the world and that they alone were beloved of Him. They felt that no other people could be God's true children and that God had written off and given up the other peoples of the world.

Some Bible teachers give the impression that God is preeminently interested in the nation of Israel and that other nations of the world are less dear to Him and less loved by Him. But the Bible emphatically declares, "God is no respecter of persons" (Acts 10:34). "But," someone objects, "were they not God's favorite people?" No. They were God's Chosen People but not His "favorite" people. God doesn't play favorites. All men are included in His great eternal love, a fact the ancient Israelites had trouble believing. The Bible assures us of God's love for everyone: "For God so loved the world, that he gave his only begotten Son, that whosoever believeth in him should not perish, but have everlasting life" (John 3:16).

Why then did God call the people of Israel to be His specially chosen people? There is no mystery at this point. The Bible makes it very plain. When God originally called Abraham, He revealed His reason for doing so: "In thee shall all families of the earth be blessed" (Gen. 12:3). On a later occasion He repeated to Abraham, "In thy seed shall all the nations of the earth be blessed; because thou hast obeyed my voice" (22:18).

He said the same thing to Jacob. "In thee and in thy seed shall all the families of the earth be blessed" (Gen. 28:14). The same had also been spoken to Isaac. The Apostle Paul tells us in the New Testament that the seed of promise was Christ (Gal. 3:16).

God Uses Human Channels

It was the purpose of God to call out these people and to use them as His instrument or channel for carrying out His plan of redemption for man. The divine purpose in the call of Abraham was not an exclusive purpose at all. It was rather an all-inclusive purpose—to bless the whole world through the Chosen People. God needed a channel through which He could preserve the knowledge of Himself among men, give His written revelation to the world, and bring His Son, Jesus Christ, into the world to be our Saviour. All these things He did through this chosen nation.

We must never lose sight of the fact that this was God's purpose in calling the nation of Israel to be His Chosen People. It was not that He loved them more than others. It was not that God has favorite people whom He wants to bless more than others. Nor was it that God had no interest in the rest of the world. It was rather that He needed a channel to carry out His plan of redemption for the whole world.

If a person studies the Old Testament carefully, He will see that God's purpose for the nation of Israel was that, through them, all the nations of the world would ultimately receive blessing. Apart from this nation, the very knowledge of God might have completely perished from among men. And how else would His Son have come into the world to provide salvation for mankind according to His eternal plan? To do all this, God needed a people who knew and obeyed Him—a people who could be His instrument in carrying out His divine purpose. Therefore, God gave to these people certain special laws which isolated them from other peoples and kept them from being contaminated by the heathenism around them.

God's prophets were sent to these people over and over again. Whenever they departed from God's way and whenever the knowledge of Him began to dim among them, God sent His prophets to call them back to the worship of the one and only true God. Through the prophets and other holy men, God gave His written revelation to these people, and through them, to the world. This was the way He carried out His scheme of redemption. It was according to this plan that the written Word of God was given to the world, the Saviour came into the world, and the Church was first established in the world.

One Divine Plan

God has only one plan, and by this plan all nations are to be blessed with the knowledge of salvation and to be given the opportunity to repent of their sins and be reconciled to their loving Creator. In the Old Testament, the nation of Israel was God's special instrument; since the Day of Pentecost, the Church has been that channel. Through the nation of Israel, God brought the Saviour into the world; but through the Church, salvation in the name of the Saviour must be proclaimed to the whole world. Through Israel, God also brought His written Word into the world; through the Church, the message of the written Word is to be proclaimed throughout the world. When we understand this, the Bible becomes much clearer to us, the Christian life becomes much more meaningful, and the significance of the Church's work is greatly increased.

Christ has come into the world. He has made atonement for sin. But now, through the Church, the message of the gospel must be proclaimed throughout the world to every creature so that whoever believes in Him will be forgiven, reconciled to God, and made a member of the Body of Jesus Christ.

Chapter 4

The Present Part of God's Plan

It is incumbent upon me to further enlarge upon the present part of this divine plan—that part which was inaugurated at the second divine intervention, the Day of Pentecost, and which is in operation now.

The Son of God, Jesus Christ, came into the world and made atonement on Calvary's cross for the sins of the world. Is it not logical, then, that the whole world should be informed of this miracle of mercy so that men might come to God through Him? And is it not logical that, since the Holy Spirit came upon the Church to empower it to fulfill the task of world evangelization, we who comprise the Church ought to be engaged in this task? Is it not reasonable to assume that since the Church is filled with the Holy Spirit and is under His divine power, it should engage itself in its primary task—preaching the gospel to every kindred, tongue, people and nation on the face of the earth? On the basis of the Scriptures, world evangelization is the logical sequence to Christ's work on Calvary and the essential result of Pentecost. And yet an honest appraisal of the Church today forces us to acknowledge that this is our weakest point and the point of our greatest failure.

World Evangelization Explained

Perhaps it is necessary at this point to emphasize exactly what "world evangelization" implies. Many earnest Christian people have thought that world evangelization means world conversion and that the task of the Church is to gradually convert men until every living person on earth receives Christ. But the Bible does not indicate that this will ever happen, nor does it require such a belief. It does not predict that through our efforts in this age, the entire world will be converted to Christ and that all men will accept Him as their Saviour and Master. Nowhere does it lead us to believe that everyone is to become a Christian through the present efforts of the Church. Yet many people have supposed this to be so, and this supposition is doubtless one of the reasons for much frustration and discouragement among Christians. Such a concept would be bound to lead to discouragement and bewilderment.

Not World Conversion

Our task is not world conversion nor even world "Christianization." There is a difference between these two: world conversion implies that every individual ultimately will become converted, whereas world Christianization suggests that Christianity will dominate the world. While the majority of Christians understand that not every individual in the world will become a Christian, many hold the view that through Christian teaching, Christian influence and the work of the Church, the world will become predominantly a Christian state or domain. They feel that through the work of world evangelization and the potent influence of the Church, such an impact will be made upon people, governments and human institutions that a virtually Christian society shall be established and hold sway over the world. They calculate that the gospel will eventually overcome wars and all social and physical ailments, making this world a place of peace, prosperity and pleasantness.

Such a concept would also, I think, lead to discouragement and frustration. If I believed that the present work of the Church was to achieve these things on a worldwide plane, I am sure I would be very discouraged, because this certainly is not being done and seemingly cannot be done. But the fact is that the Bible predicts that wars, abounding iniquities, troubles, perplexities, injustices, and tribulations of all kinds will be with us to the very end of this age, even increasing as we draw near to the end. So let us not be deceived, troubled or perplexed.

It should be further emphasized that neither is it God's plan or His assignment to us to establish the kingdom of heaven on earth by our present efforts. The kingdom of heaven will never actually be established on earth by the Church's program and efforts. When Jesus taught His disciples to pray, He said, "After this manner therefore pray ye: . . . Thy kingdom come. Thy will be done in earth, as it is in heaven" (Matt. 6:9,10). The term He used in outlining this model prayer does not mean a gradual coming of the kingdom through an operational process; it implies a sudden coming or a sudden appearing of Jesus' visible kingdom and earthly power. This is what He told us to pray for.

Our task now, as Christians, is to preach the gospel throughout the world and to proclaim repentance and remission of sins in the name of Christ among all the nations. All the while we are doing this we are to pray constantly for the coming of Christ, who will personally return to earth and set up His own glorious kingdom of righteousness and peace in this world.

Christians' Misunderstanding

Jesus' disciples had previously failed to understand His teaching concerning the kingdom. He had pointed out to them that it was written that He would have to suffer and die for the sins of the world and be raised from the dead (Luke 24:46). He had also told them they must preach repentance and remission of sins in His name among all the nations. But they asked Him just before His ascension, "Lord, wilt thou at this time restore again the kingdom to Israel?" (Acts 1:6). They were obsessed with the idea of the restoration of the Davidic kingdom then and there. They wanted to see the kingdom of heaven set up on earth immediately. But Jesus responded to this by saying, in effect, "No, that is not God's present program. It is not for you to know the time for that. The Father has chosen not to reveal that plan. The kingdom will come in due time. I will return in the Father's own time and establish that kingdom upon earth. But this is not your task."

These disciples didn't really understand God's plan. Before Jesus went to the cross, they obviously did not understand what He had come to do at that time. Even after He had been raised from the dead, they still didn't understand the next part of the divine plan. After their enlightenment concerning the Scriptures, they came to an understanding of the first part—that Christ had to suffer and to rise from the dead in order to provide redemption for the souls of men. But not until after Pentecost did they understand the second part—that it was their task to preach repentance and remission of sins throughout the world.

Since the establishment of the kingdom on earth was not Jesus' next step after the cross, what then was His next step? He said to His disciples, "Ye shall receive power, after that the Holy Ghost is come upon you: and ye shall be witnesses unto me both in Jerusalem, and in all Judaea, and in Samaria, and unto the uttermost part of the earth" (Acts 1:8). This meant the evangelization of the entire world. As I have stated, this does not mean world conversion, it does not mean world Christianization, and it does not mean the establishment of the kingdom of God upon earth now. What it does mean is the preaching of the good news of redemption and remission of sins in the name of Christ throughout all the world.

God Is Visiting the Nations

The Apostle James made a significant statement in the Jerusalem Church Council, which delineated God's plan for the present age. God has begun to visit the nations, he declared, quoting Peter, "to take out of them a people for his name" (Acts 15:14). This is God's present plan. Through world evangelization and through the work of the Holy Spirit attending the preaching of the gospel, God is gathering out of all the nations "a people for his name." He is making up the true Church, the Body of Jesus Christ. And it is His plan that this Church shall be constituted of human beings redeemed out of every part of the earth, out of every segment of the human family, and from every race, color, kindred, tribe and nation. The song that the redeemed will sing in heaven is recorded in the vision of the Apostle John in Revelation 5: "Thou wast slain, and hast redeemed us to God by thy blood out of every kindred, and tongue, and people, and nation" (v. 9).

This is God's plan and purpose, and this is what He is doing in the world today. Through the proclamation of the gospel of Jesus Christ, God is visiting the nations of the world. He is gathering out of these nations those who respond to the message of repentance and remission of sins through Jesus Christ and are reconciled to God by faith in Him. All of these become members of Christ's Body, and thus God is completing that Body.

Let us not be deceived. Neither let us be troubled, perplexed or doubtful. Our assignment is not to convert the world. Our task is not to make

35

the whole world essentially Christian. Our task is not to produce the kingdom of heaven on earth by our efforts. If it were, we could only feel discouraged and bewildered in an hour like this.

Then what is our task? It is to make the gospel of Jesus Christ known to all men. God's plan demands that the gospel be preached among all the nations, and by this means He gathers out a people for His Son's name. This is our task, and this is God's divine plan—preaching the gospel to the whole world. This is the divine purpose, and this purpose is being carried out.

God's plan and purpose in the world is not being defeated. It cannot be defeated. But we must be sure that we understand exactly what that plan and purpose is. Through personal witness and the preaching of the gospel, by means of radio and literature and many other methods available to us today, God is carrying out His plan of world evangelization and completing the Body of His Son, Jesus Christ, which Body is the Church.

Chapter 5

A New Consciousness of God's Power

In addition to a true understanding of God's plan for the world, discussed in Chapter 4, a desperate need among us as Christians today is for a new consciousness of God's power.

Paul's Apostolic Prayer

In the first chapter of the Epistle to the Ephesians, where God's eternal purpose is mentioned, God is described as the One "who worketh all things after the counsel of his own will" (Eph. 1:11). It is highly significant that in the same chapter the Apostle Paul prays that Christians might know "what is the exceeding greatness of his power to us-ward who believe, according to the working of his mighty power, which he wrought in Christ, when he raised him from the dead, and set him at his own right hand in the heavenly places" (vv. 19,20).

Paul positively refers to God's eternal plan and purpose in Jesus Christ in both chapters 1 and 3 of his Ephesian letter, and he prays that these

37

believers might know the exceeding greatness of God's power toward them. Obviously we need not only an understanding of His divine plan but also a true awareness of His divine power to enable us, as His instruments, to fulfill that part of the plan which is incumbent upon us.

Jesus put His finger on the vital place when He said to the people of His day, "Do ye not therefore err, because ye know not the scriptures, neither the power of God?" (Mark 12:24). This declaration was the actual indictment, not the statement which followed it, "Ye therefore do greatly err" (v. 27). These people were guilty of two errors. They had misunderstood the Scriptures. Therefore they did not understand God's purpose and plan in sending the Messiah; neither did they understand or know the power of God. There are some Christian people who do mentally comprehend God's plan. They know that His plan calls for total evangelization of the world, but they stumble at the barriers and difficulties that stand in the way of doing this. Some openly say, "It is impossible to evangelize the whole world and to preach the gospel to all the people of the earth." Even Christian leaders frequently declare disbelief in the possibility of the task.

Jesus' Promise

But we must not forget that, when the Lord Jesus gave the Great Commission to His disciples to go into all the world and preach the gospel to every creature, He also promised them His all-enabling, divine power. In the Gospel of Matthew He is recorded as having said, "All power is given unto me in heaven and in earth. Go ye therefore, . . . and, lo, I am with you alway" (28:18-20). After Jesus had told His disciples, "As my Father hath sent me, even so send I you" (John 20:21), He breathed on them and said, "Receive ye the Holy Ghost" (v. 22). This was the power!

Chapter 24 of the Gospel of Luke records His words: "It is written, and thus it behoved Christ to suffer, and to rise from the dead the third day: and that repentance and remission of sins should be preached in His name among all nations, beginning at Jerusalem. And ye are witnesses of these things. . . . But tarry ye in the city of Jerusalem, until ye be endued with power from on high" (vv. 46-49).

Notice that in all of these passages the Great Commission of Jesus to His disciples to launch into a program of worldwide evangelization was accompanied by His divine promise of essential spiritual power. It is for this reason that I must emphasize this fact—we need today not only a comprehension of His divine plan but also a consciousness of His divine power.

The classic passage dealing with the Spirit's power for worldwide witness is the first chapter of the Book of Acts. Jesus said, "John truly baptized with water; but ye shall be baptized with the Holy Ghost not many days hence. When they therefore were come together, they asked of him, saying, Lord, wilt thou at this time restore again the kingdom to Israel? And he said unto them, It is not for you to know the times or the seasons which the Father hath put in his own power. But ye shall receive power, after that the Holy Ghost is come upon you: and ye shall be witnesses unto me both in Jerusalem, and in all Judaea, and in Samaria, and unto the uttermost part of the earth" (vv. 5-8).

This is a most vital passage of Holy Scripture. It is well known to Christians everywhere, but perhaps it is not as well understood as supposed. Two great things are seen here: a clarification of God's divine plan and the verification of His divine power, the power of the Holy Spirit. These disciples, who still did not fully comprehend God's purpose, asked Jesus if He was going to restore the earthly kingdom immediately. Jesus replied, in essence, "No, not now. In the Father's time that will take place. But right now His plan is for you to be witnesses of my saving grace to the uttermost part of the earth, starting right at Jerusalem."

Spirit's Power Available

This clarified the divine plan in the minds and hearts of these disciples with the result that, after the Day of Pentecost, they gave themselves without reservation to the task of preaching the gospel everywhere to the people of their generation. But, as I have just stated, this passage also verifies the fact that divine power was available.

Both of these factors are exceedingly important. We must clearly comprehend what God's divine plan is, and we must also be clearly conscious of the divine power at our disposal to fulfill that plan. We need not throw up our hands in despair and say it is impossible. Instead, we need to become conscious of the all-sufficient power of the Holy Spirit and claim that power in our lives and activities.

40

Jesus made that promise to His disciples because He knew they could not carry out the Great Commission on their own. And they knew it too. They knew that the task He had assigned to them was far beyond their own power or ability. Therefore they waited in the city of Jerusalem, as He had instructed them, for the Spirit's coming.

"These all continued with one accord in prayer and supplication" (Acts 1:14). In that upper room in the city they waited and prayed for the coming of the Holy Spirit, knowing that His coming would bring them the required power to fulfill the command Jesus had so recently given them. On the Day of Pentecost they experienced the coming of that divine power. When the Holy Spirit came upon them that day, they were filled with His power. They spoke with divine authority. They were even given power to preach the gospel in the languages of all the various peoples that were represented there that day. Thousands had come from all over the world to celebrate the Feast of Pentecost, and the disciples spoke in the languages of all those people. And they spoke with mighty convicting and converting power. Three thousand persons were converted to Jesus Christ in that one day! It was then that the work of world evangelization was launched.

The power of God in the Person of the Holy Spirit came that day to abide in the Church and to make it His dwelling place and His temple, but above all, His instrument. From that day forward these men depended solely on the Spirit's power for their work of evangelizing. We read again and again in the early chapters of Acts that they were filled with the Holy Spirit.

Power in the Early Church

Not only were these men constantly "on the go" with the gospel, the Holy Spirit gave them added power and ability to launch out in the name of Christ and to boldly preach the gospel to people everywhere. Nothing could stop these men. Nothing could deter them. Nothing could slow them up. Threats, imprisonments, suffering, persecution—nothing that men could employ against them could stop them from preaching the gospel of Jesus Christ to their generation. Their enemies were confounded. The lives of multitudes of people were transformed. Whole communities were changed. Churches were established that soon flourished. We read: "The word of God grew and multiplied" (Acts 12:24) and "The Lord added to the church daily such as should be saved [those that were being saved]" (2:47). Victory followed victory in that first century.

It was said of those early Christian witnesses that they "turned the world upside down" (17:6). Heathen altars were forsaken, pagan temples were deserted, and idols and pagan relics were publicly burned in the cities.

This was not done by the power of men; it was done by the unlimited power of the Spirit of God, and even the enemies of the early Christians had to acknowledge this fact. Rabbi Gamaliel in Jerusalem warned the Sanhedrin that these men could be possessed with the power of God, and he cautioned, "Take heed to yourselves what ye intend to do as touching [concerning] these men. . . . Lest haply ye be found even to fight against God" (Acts 5:35,39). These men were filled with a spiritual power which both they themselves and all their opposers recognized and acknowledged.

They had few human advantages. Their practical discernment was limited. They were not men of great learning or great influence. They certainly were not men of wealth. They did not rank high in the social strata of their day, and they were not considered to be men of culture. They had but little behind them in the way of church organization. They had none of the facilities and equipment we have today. But they were aware of the power of God in their lives, and they allowed the Holy Spirit to use them mightily as His own instruments.

This is what is needed in the Church today. We need a new consciousness and a new claiming of this divine power in order that we may launch forward in a mighty new surge of worldwide evangelization, following the divine plan marked out for us in the Scriptures.

Those early Christian witnesses went out as flaming messengers of the gospel of Jesus Christ. They preached to their generation the message of the crucified and risen Saviour and salvation through personal faith in Him. That was true not only in the early church but also throughout the first several centuries of the Christian era.

Later Declension

In order that we might profit from the solemn lesson set forth, we must note that as expansion and prosperity, along with institutional strength and power, began to characterize the new entity known as "the church," it no longer fit the New Testament definition of "the Church," the Body of Christ. People began to rely on "the church" and its power and prestige rather than fully depending on the divine power of the Holy Spirit.

As an institution, "the church" grew and multiplied until it ultimately achieved great intellectual power. Brilliant men came into the church and became its key leaders. The people in the church began to rely on these intellectual leaders and gradually lost the sense of utter reliance upon the power of the Holy Spirit which had marked the first century. They trusted in their brilliant apologists. More and more they leaned on their leaders, on their well-devised church creeds, and on the organized councils, where learned leaders met together to make decisions and devise new creeds. As brilliant men rose to the front and to the top, the effects of the Holy Spirit's power were gradually diminished. The church gained great intellectural power, but in the subtle gaining of intellectual power it lost her spiritual power. A study of Church History attests to this.

The church also achieved great organizational power with the passing of time. In the early church there was little organization and virtually no organizational power. As the need seemed to rise, organization increased. But in the work of God there is always a danger that as organization grows and increases in strength, we tend to depend on that kind of power and lose our consciousness and dependence on the power of the Holy Spirit. This is clearly what happened in the church after the first couple of centuries. The church ultimately became a gigantic ecclesiastical organization with

44

great efficiency and strength. And the ecclesiastical organization asserted its power in all directions.

As the ecclesiastical organization came to the fore and wielded power, the true power of God was gradually withdrawn. People began to rely on the church as a great organization and as a great ecclesiastical power, and they leaned less and less on the power of God. The early church had very little organization and no ecclesiastical power, but it had an astonishing spiritual power. The later church had great organizational power but very little spiritual power.

The organized church in due time also achieved great financial strength. The early church at first had no such thing as economic power. The saints in Jerusalem were so poverty stricken that the Apostle Paul, the first missionary to the Gentiles, collected gifts from the Gentile churches in other countries to help the Christians in Jerusalem. That was quite the opposite of our modern procedure of gathering money from the churches in the homeland to send to pagan areas. This was "missionary giving in reverse"! Later, however, the church achieved vast economic resources.

As organization grew and as powerful leaders in the church increased, riches also increased and the church ultimately became exceedingly wealthy. It became involved and interested in real estate, gaining possession of valuable properties, erecting magnificent buildings, and so on. Beautiful and costly cathedrals became the centers of attraction and interest, and the people began to look to their beautiful buildings and expensive places of worship instead of relying on the power of God. And as they became more and more enamored by the great temples and cathedrals, they lost the consciousness that individual believers themselves were the real temples of the Holy Spirit. As this glorious consciousness receded, individual believers likewise lost their sense of mission in the world and their sense of spiritual obligation, service and witness. They relied on the church to do the work of God; the individual finally was considered to be of little importance. It was the great ecclesiastical institution, the church, that would monopolize the work of God. The more the church achieved in the way of material wealth, the poorer it grew spiritually.

In the course of time the church also gained great political power and became intricately involved in political affairs and in government. The leaders of the church became political leaders with loud state voices. Political involvement gripped the church harder and harder, and as this happened the grip of the Holy Spirit was felt less and less. Political affairs finally seemed to permeate and control the church, and the church, in turn, finally got control of the political affairs. Outwardly it may have appeared that "the church" was making a great impact on the world and was being very successful, but the spiritual power it needed was little sought and finally lost.

Effect on Missionary Effort

Meanwhile, what about missionary work? What became of world evangelization? As the church gained in intellectual power, organizational power, economic power and political power, the work of missions—what little was being done—was largely

46

an expression of "churchianity." It was guided by human measures and human goals, and it was achieved by human means. In fact, for the most part, true missionary vision perished from the church, and the so-called missionary work that was carried on by individuals from time to time was largely a great ecclesiastical program rather than a sincere effort to win men to Jesus Christ. Of course, we do thank God for those true, faithful and loyal men all through the centuries who maintained a genuine missionary vision and gave themselves to the preaching of the gospel in other lands. There were always some who did this.

But today we see a great deal of power in the church that is not necessarily true spiritual power. We observe great intellectual power in Christendom and, more than we should, we rely on our brilliant and intellectual leaders. Thank God for every brilliant, intellectual, well-educated man who has found Jesus Christ as his Saviour and who is using his talents, his knowledge and his ability in the work of Christ. But it is a sad day for the Church when it depends on the brains of men instead of on the power of the Holy Spirit to fulfill its mission in the world. This is a real danger in our day, for it is the tendency of our times. We need a new visitation of divine power—a new consciousness of that power and a new experience of that power—because as these other powers in the Church increase, spiritual power tends to decline and sometimes to disappear. The Holy Spirit has had to write the word "Ichabod" ("the glory is departed," I Sam. 4:21) over some of our Christian institutions.

The Church today has a good deal of organizational power. We thank God for all true Christian organizations, and we recognize the need for them. But we must not depend on organized religion instead of on the Spirit's power.

Political power and a place in secular government do not constitute God's role for the Church in this dispensation.

There is certainly a strong tendency and a subtle danger among us to depend on material wealth—our wonderful buildings and the other material possessions belonging to churches and church-related institutions. These are all good in their place, but if they ever take the place of the conscious power of the Holy Spirit among us, they become terrible stumbling blocks and deterrents.

Therefore I repeat, we need among us today a new consciousness of divine power and a new ability to claim that power in our lives. We need a new comprehension of God's plan and an understanding of just what He is doing in the world and what He wants us to do. But even more than that, we need a new consciousness, a new awareness and a new experience and visitation of the divine power of His Holy Spirit among us.

Chapter 6

A New Conviction of Man's Need

"In the beginning was the Word, and the Word was with God, and the Word was God. The same was in the beginning with God. In him was life; and the life was the light of men. And the light shineth in darkness; and the darkness comprehended it not. That was the true Light, which lighteth every man that cometh into the world" (John 1:1,2,4,5,9).

We have already pointed out that Christians today need a new consciousness of God's plan for the world. We need to know exactly what He is seeking to achieve in the world. We also need a new consciousness of God's divine power—a consciousness of the power and presence of the Holy Spirit working in us.

Men Apart From Christ are Lost

Let us consider another vital need in modern Christendom. We need a new conviction of man's need—a conviction of the fact that men need to hear about Jesus Christ in order to know God and in order to be reconciled to Him in saving faith. Many Christians lack a conviction about the lost state of men who have no knowledge of Jesus

49

Christ. Yet the Bible unequivocally declares that apart from Him, men are in darkness; apart from Him, there is no spiritual light or life and no hope of salvation. Jesus Himself said that He came into the world "to seek and to save that which was lost" (Luke 19:10). If men were not lost, there would be no necessity for Christ to save them. Had it not been for the fact that men, by virtue of their sin, were cut off from God and lost for time and eternity, He never would have come into the world to seek and save them.

In Luke 15 we read several parables Jesus gave teaching the fact that men are lost. In the parable of the lost sheep He shows that men without Him are like sheep astray from the shepherd and separated from the fold. In the story of the lost coin He teaches more concerning the lost condition of man. Then He gives the parable of the lost son, the young man who went far away from his father's presence and house and became a defeated victim of sin. The youth was lost, separated from his father, degraded and perishing with hunger, but he went back home. By means of such parables and other clear teaching, Jesus revealed that He came to seek and to restore lost humanity to God.

The Apostle Paul said that our gospel is "hid to them that are lost: in whom the god of this world [Satan] hath blinded the minds of them which believe not" (II Cor. 4:3,4). The Bible asserts that men who are without Christ have no hope and are without God in the world (Eph. 2:12). We are told that they are "alienated from the life of God through the ignorance that is in them [spiritual ignorance, ignorance of the gospel] because of the blindness of their heart" (4:18).

Yet many Christians keep saying, "If the heathen are sincere in what they believe, will they not be saved, even if they do not follow the right religion?" Others say, "Will God not accept the worship of pagans who do not know the truth, and will they not be saved on account of their ignorance?" On such a knotty pillow Christians try to rest their careless heads and pacify their consciences. Some even say, "Those people who have never heard the gospel are happy and satisfied in their heathen religions which, after all, are suited to them. So why not leave them alone?

A Present Plight

This is why I assert and emphasize, on the basis of the authority of the Bible, that we need among us, as Christians today, a new conviction of the lost condition of men—a new conviction of human plight and need apart from Christ. First, we need to be aware of the fact that right now, in their present state, men are separated from God by virtue of their sin. It isn't just that men will be lost in eternity—they are lost now. This is their present plight. This is their condition and need now.

Jesus said, "I am the light of the world: he that followeth me shall not walk in darkness, but shall have the light of life" (John 8:12). In such statements the assumption is clear that apart from Him all men are in spiritual darkness. Is this a valid claim? Is Jesus Christ the only real light of the world? Is it true that unless men follow Him they are not following the light? Is it true that those who do not know Him and follow Him are in spiritual darkness?

If Christ's claim is not valid, His assertion that only those who follow Him have light and all others walk in darkness would mark Him as a terrible deceiver and imposter. But if His claim is true, then men must either come to know and follow Him or abide in eternal spiritual darkness. Few, if any, readers of this book have any doubt that Jesus is the true Saviour, nor do they believe that He is an imposter. But we must face up to the fact that if He is indeed the true light of the world, then men must come to know Him or they are in darkness. The Bible consistently affirms this gripping fact: In Christ alone is spiritual life to be found, and apart from Him men are lost in darkness and death.

In John 1 we are told that in Christ was life, and this life was the light of men, and that this light shines on in the darkness, and the darkness has never been able to overcome it. This passage clearly states that He is the true light who came into the world to illuminate every man. Jesus Christ came to bring light to all the world and into the life and soul of every human being. He came "to give light to them that sit in darkness and in the shadow of death" (Luke 1:79).

The aged prophet Simeon was in the temple in Jerusalem when Joseph and Mary took the infant Jesus there to be circumcised. Simeon proclaimed Him "a light to lighten the Gentiles, and the glory of [God's] people Israel" (Luke 2:32). The Apostle Paul testified that the Lord Jesus Christ had sent him to the heathen "to open their eyes, and to turn them from darkness to light, and from the power of Satan unto God" (Acts 26:18). This certainly means that before He came to them with the light of the gospel, they were in darkness, they were blinded, and they were held under the power of Satan, the god of this world.

In John 6:17 there is a striking statement concerning an incident which took place during Jesus' earthly life. It embraces a deep spiritual lesson: "It was now dark, and Jesus was not come to them." While this is a mere historical statement of fact, it illustrates a vital spiritual truth, because where Jesus has not come, men are indeed in darkness. All men are in total spiritual darkness until the light of Jesus Christ comes to them. Without Christ they are in moral darkness, social darkness and spiritual darkness. The great tragedy and the sad plight of the whole world today is that men either do not know or do not desire to follow the Son of God, who is the light of life.

Without Hope for the Future

Second, we need to realize not only that men apart from Christ are separated from God but also that they face eternal perdition. Their present status of being lost in spiritual darkness and of being separated from God will become an eternal plight unless they come to know the Saviour, Christ Jesus. There is no salvation apart from Him. Ephesians 2:12 declares that men who are without Christ are without hope and without God.

Jesus, in His prayer to the Heavenly Father, said, "This is life eternal, that they might know thee the only true God, and Jesus Christ, whom thou hast sent" (John 17:3). Prior to this He plainly said to His disciples, "I am the way, the truth, and the life: no man cometh unto the

Father, but by me" (14:6). So it is true that not only are men now separated from God, not only are they now lost in darkness, not only are they now under the power of sin, but unless they come to know salvation through Jesus Christ, they will be eternally separated from God—forever lost. They will be eternally held in chains of darkness and the power of the prince of darkness.

"For God so loved the world, that he gave his only begotten Son, that whosoever believeth in him should not perish, but have everlasting life" (John 3:16). These familiar words clearly imply that those who do not believe in Him, who do not know Him, and who do not trust Him, will not have everlasting life but will perish forever.

When Jesus opened the understanding of His disciples concerning the Scriptures, He said, "Thus it is written, and thus it behoved Christ to suffer, and to rise from the dead the third day: and that repentance and remission of sins should be preached in his name among all nations" (Luke 24:46,47). Christ died on the cross for the sins of the world; but the message of repentance and remission of sins must be preached so that men can be saved. Repentance from sin and personal faith in Jesus Christ are requisites of eternal salvation.

Need for a New Attitude

Most certainly in our day we need a new conviction of the lostness and hopelessness of men outside of Jesus Christ. Without such a change in attitude none of us will be greatly disturbed about those who have not heard the gospel. Missionary work is not likely to be taken very seriously, and it will never claim very much sacrificial participation. If I could believe that men could somehow find their way to God and be saved from the eternal penalty of their sins without hearing the gospel, I don't think I would be very much troubled about it either. But I believe what the Bible teaches—that men who are without Christ are without hope, both for now and for eternity. Because of this, I feel we can leave no stone unturned in the endeavor to get the message of Jesus Christ to the world. To this endeavor I have dedicated my life, and I urge you to read and study your Bible with an open heart on this vital matter. If you do so, I think you, too, will see that apart from Christ there is no hope for human salvation.

Have you ever faced the fact that men need to hear the gospel in order to be saved? Have you ever faced the challenge of dedicating your life to Christ and being willing to go anywhere He might send you to take the light of the gospel to those who still have never heard? May God grant us the conviction in our souls concerning what His Word teaches—that men must know of Christ—and may we willingly go anywhere He may send us and do anything He may ask us to do so that men who are now in darkness might come to His light.

Chapter 7

A New Compulsion of Divine Love

"Though I speak with the tongues of men and of angels, and have not charity [love], I am become as sounding brass, or a tinkling cymbal. And though I have the gift of prophecy, and understand all mysteries, and all knowledge; and though I have all faith, so that I could remove mountains, and have not charity [love], I am nothing. And though I bestow all my goods to feed the poor, and though I give my body to be burned, and have not charity [love], it profiteth me nothing" (I Cor. 13:1-3).

"For through the Holy Spirit that has been given us, God's love has flooded our hearts" (Rom. 5:5, Williams).

In addition to what we have thus far considered as being desperately needed among us as Christians today, we have a great need for a new compulsion of divine love within us and among us.

In our churches there are certain people who "talk about" missions and even "agitate for" missions, but not always do they do this with genuine love and compassion. I have known of certain individuals who agitated for a missionary program in their churches with sheer carnal bitterness and even anger. Perhaps they thought they were being motivated by a true missionary burden, whereas they may simply have been motivated by some lesser obsession. But a missionary program activated by human agitation or irritation or ire cannot be acceptable to God. In fact, it may do more to defeat than to further a real missionary program in the church. Such motives grieve the Spirit of God and receive resistance from the people of the church.

No doubt we have all heard people pray that the Lord would give them "a burden for souls." But the way they use the word "souls" gives the impression that they regard souls in some abstract sense and indicates that they really do not know what they are asking God for. Some of the very people who so often pray for a "burden for souls" dislike or even despise certain people and certain groups of peoples. Obviously we need something more than this!

The Power of Divine Compassion

We need a new compulsion of divine love. There is no greater power in all the world than the power of love. Love will drive people and enable them to do what nothing else can cause or compel them to do. The Bible well declares, "Love is strong as death" (Song of Sol. 8:6). Death is one power that is universally recognized as superseding all human power. We are well aware that man has no power in his hands as strong as the power of death, and we know that human power cannot defeat death. With all our knowledge of medical science and with all we have learned about human existence and the human body, we are still helpless before the power of death. Quite often one hears the statement that the two surest things in life are death and taxes. Death, of course, is surer than taxes: some people manage to avoid paying taxes, but no one can avoid death.

In the New Testament we are told, "In Jesus Christ neither circumcision availeth any thing, nor uncircumcision; but faith which worketh by love" (Gal. 5:6). Notice that expression, "Faith . . . worketh by love [in love]." All true faith works by love, and in love. The faith that is not accompanied by love—by loving ministry and loving service—is, according to the Apostle James, vain and dead (James 2:17). But true faith works in love. There is no greater incentive to do anything than the incentive of genuine love. And this must be the one underlying incentive for foreign missionary endeavor.

Why is it that the true Church of Christ is doing so little, comparatively speaking, toward getting the gospel to the unreached tribes in the dark and needy areas of the earth? Is it not because we lack the compulsion of divine love? This is the one essential underlying motive that must be present in the Christian's heart and in the Church in order to accomplish the evangelization of the world.

By Love Compelled

Rather than generalizing about love, we must be specific. Therefore I wish to specify just how it

58

is that love compels us, as Christians, to go to the ends of the earth with the gospel of Jesus Christ.

By Love Compelled, a book written by Marshall Broomhall and published in 1936 by the China Inland Mission, tells the story of that great missionary society now known as the Overseas Missionary Fellowship. It chronicles the lives of the men and women who went to China in the early days and who suffered so many things and sacrificed so much because they were "by love compelled." Because of the compulsion of love, no suffering was too intense and no sacrifice was too great for those pioneers. They gladly suffered and sacrificed in order to proclaim the message of Christ to those needy people—because they were compelled by the divine love of God.

There are at least three ways in which love compels us to become involved in missions. First of all, the realization and contemplation of Christ's love to us becomes a mighty compulsion to make His salvation known to others and to seek to bring them to Him. Isaac Watts, the famed 18th-century poet, wrote:

When I survey the wondrous cross
   On which the Prince of glory died,
My richest gain I count but loss,
   And pour contempt on all my pride.

Were the whole realm of nature mine,
   That were a present far too small:
Love so amazing, so divine,
   Demands my soul, my life, my all.

59

This was the experience of a man who contemplated the love of Christ to him and who came to realize how great that love was. He said that even if he owned the whole world, that would be insufficient payment to Christ for His redeeming love. Note his words: "Love so amazing, so divine, demands my soul, my life, my all." Certainly all who contemplate and truly comprehend the greatness of Christ's love to us must be compelled to echo his words. Such amazing, divine love does indeed demand body and soul and all that we are and possess.

Jesus said, "Greater love hath no man than this, that a man lay down his life for his friends" (John 15:13). He laid down His life on Calvary's cross for us, He left the ivory palaces of heaven and came into this world of woe; He became a man of sorrows and acquainted with grief; He bore our sins in His own body; and He suffered all the shame and agony of Calvary in order to make atonement for our sins. He did all of this because He loved us so much. That is the only explanation there is. Our finite minds cannot understand how Christ would do this for us except for the fact that He loved us with such great love. When we fully realize the depth of that love, we cast ourselves before His feet in utter and complete surrender and say, "Lord, here is my life, here are my treasures, here are my ambitions, here are my plans, here is my all. I surrender everything to Your will. What wilt Thou have me to do?"

After the mother of my children passed away, I heard my younger daughter say to her older sister one day, "Whenever I realized that I had hurt Mother, it just about killed me." This girl had known the greatness of her mother's love to her, and she testified that whenever she had displeased or injured her mother in any way by disobedience, it made her most unhappy. This is the way of love. When we fully realize the intensity and the depth of the love of Christ for us, we should be affected the same way. It should make us utterly miserable to know we have displeased or grieved Him.

I'm sure the one thing that would please our Saviour more than anything else would be for us to endeavor to fulfill the last great command He gave to His apostles and, through them, to the Church: "Go ye into all the world, and preach the gospel to every creature" (Mark 16:15).

Truly we need a new compulsion of divine love, and this will come to us through a contemplation and realization of the greatness of God's love for us.

Love for Christ

Another facet of this matter concerning the compulsion of divine love needs to be cited and emphasized: Our love for Him, if it is real and genuine, will become a compelling force in us to seek the lost and to plead with them to be reconciled to God through faith in Jesus Christ. Simply stated, our love for Christ will be a compulsion within us, causing us to obey His commandments and to preach His gospel throughout the world. He said so Himself. "If ye love me," He told His disciples, "keep my commandments" (John 14:15). Paraphrased, He was saying, "If you have a true, genuine love for Me, your love for Me will be a compulsion within

61

you to obey My commandments." Jesus didn't give very many commandments to His Church, but one commandment which He did give was to preach His gospel to all the world. He commanded His disciples to begin at Jerusalem on the Day of Pentecost and to go on and on until they had reached the ends of the earth with the witness of His gospel.

The Holy Spirit adds further testimony to this in other portions of the Scriptures. In I John we find a statement very similar to the one made by Jesus Himself: "By this we know that we love the children of God, when we love God, and keep His commandments. For this is the love of God, that we keep His commandments: and His commandments are not grievous" (5:2,3). Here it is affirmed that when we love God, we keep His commandments. This is indeed the way and nature of love.

If I really love my God and if I really adore my Saviour as I profess to, there will be within me a driving force leading me to do all within my power to obey and fulfill His commandments. These commandments, according to John, are not grievous. No commandment is ever grievous when love is involved. If you are forced to obey someone you do not love, obedience becomes a very hard and grievous task. But it is never grievous nor difficult to obey a person you·love. It is not grievous for children to obey their parents when family members love one another. Nor is it difficult for a missionary to obey the command of Christ to go to the ends of the earth to preach the gospel when he truly loves the Saviour.

People who really love Jesus don't think of the "burden" of foreign missions or about the "sacrifice" involved. They are "by love compelled," and love takes the burden and the grief out of the task. But those who are motivated by any less noble incentive than love will naturally think in terms of sacrifice.

A mother who loves her children doesn't think of the great sacrifice required on her part to raise those children and care for them. A woman who loves her husband doesn't talk about the sacrifice of being his wife and living to please him. A man who loves and cares for his wife doesn't care about the sacrifices he has to make to provide for her and support her. Marriage, though it involves a certain legal bondage, is properly a bondage of love. Any who go to the marriage altar with the idea that they will henceforth have to "sacrifice" much would be better off single.

The Apostle Paul was a man who truly loved Jesus Christ, and out of the experience of his own heart he said, "The love of Christ constraineth us" (II Cor. 5:14). This love compelled him or inwardly forced him to do God's will and to live for Him rather than for himself.

To know Jesus Christ truly, is to love Him; to love Him is to serve Him; and to serve Him is to make His gospel known to needy men everywhere. How can a person who truly loves the Saviour be indifferent to a lost world? How can a person who truly loves Christ be indifferent to His command to evangelize the world?

His Love in Us

The third fact to be emphasized is that Christ's love in us—His own divine love imparted to us and implanted in us—gives us a burden for the souls of men and impels us to go to them with the message of salvation.

To crystallize in our minds the role of love in motivating us for evangelism, let us summarize: First, the realization of God's love to us compels us to go to the ends of the earth; second, our love for God, if it is genuine, compels us to please Him by sharing the gospel; and third, God's own love, imparted to us and implanted in us, burdens us for the souls of those who are in darkness and makes us desire to go to them with the message of life and hope.

Remember that the Apostle Paul, who, because the love of Christ for his own people consumed him, said, "I could wish that myself were accursed from Christ for my brethren" (Rom. 9:3). He also said, "I have great heaviness and continual sorrow in my heart" (v. 2). This man was constantly burdened for his own people and testified, "My heart's desire and prayer to God for Israel is, that they might be saved" (10:1). This was not merely a natural love in the heart of a normal man; it was the divine love of God implanted in the heart of a spiritual man. Paul wrote: "The love of God is shed abroad in our hearts by the Holy Ghost which is given unto us" (5:5). Love is indeed the very first evidence of the fruit of the Spirit (Gal. 5:22,23), and any person who is filled with the Spirit is filled with the love of God. The two experiences must and always will go together.

David Brainerd, who was one of the earliest men to carry the gospel to the primitive Indians of North America, was found one morning on his knees in his wigwam in sub-zero weather. But perspiration was dripping off his face as he cried out to God for the souls of the Indians he had learned to love and sought to win for Christ. He was compelled by love in his own heart, put there by the Holy Spirit. It was said of Hudson Taylor, "The sun never rose on China without finding Taylor on his knees." Doing what? Crying out to God for the souls of the people in that great land. Such actions were not natural; they were due to the love of God implanted in the soul of a man of God.

This is exactly what it takes to make a missionary. Human love alone cannot do it. The contemplation of Christ's love to us may not itself be sufficient. Our love to Him may fall short. But God's own love, implanted within our hearts by the Holy Ghost, is sufficient to drive us anywhere to proclaim the gospel of Christ to men.

It is this, the love of God shed forth into our hearts, that takes the "ice" out of "sacrifice" and leaves only the "sacra"; that is, the sacred. It is this that takes the "shun" out of "evangelization." It makes world evangelization a privilege rather than a burden or a duty. It is this that takes the "irk" out of missionary "work" and the "bore" out of missionary "labor" for Christ. And for all who labor in behalf of missions, this puts a capital "L" on "life." When a person is filled with the Holy Spirit and with the divine love of God, he lives life to the fullest.

It was Christ's love that moved Him to come into this world and to go to the cross to provide salvation for sinful man. And it must be His love in us that moves us to take up that cross and bear it to the ends of the earth for His name.

Without Love, Nothing

Without the divine love of God implanted in us, missionary work would largely be in vain. Such work would neither bring deep inward satisfaction to us nor very much blessing to others. Nor would it bring true joy to the heart of our Saviour. The Apostle Paul realized this when he wrote: "Though I give my body to be burned, and have not charity [love], it profiteth me nothing" (I Cor. 13:3). As Christians today, we need a new compulsion of divine love. We must have a realization of God's love to us, a response of love to Him, and above all, His own divine love filling our hearts through the Holy Spirit, who has been given to us.

We need to pray that the Holy Spirit may fill us with His divine love. This is one of our greatest needs today.

Chapter 8

A New Confrontation
With Opportunities

In addition to the things thus far pointed out, I feel that Christians in this generation need to have a new confrontation with the opportunities that face them.

Many are saying, "The doors are closing to missionaries all over the world." Some are also saying, "The day of the foreign missionary is about ended. Foreign missionary work is coming to an end." I have heard some people say, "Athiestic Communism is irrevocably sweeping over the whole world and will soon stop all Christian activity." Still others are saying, "There is no longer a need for American missionaries overseas, and there is little opportunity for them anyway."

It is true that certain doors are closed. The political door of Russia is closed. The same is true of some other countries, like mainland China, Cuba, Sudan, Mauretania, and so on.

In contrast to all of this I must point out that we need to honestly confront the great opportunities that do face Christians today all around the world—opportunities greater than any ever faced in the history of the Church. There are some doors that men cannot close.

Instead of lamenting the closed doors, we should face the challenge of the ones that are wide open and remember Christ's great promises and the provisions He gave with His command to evangelize the world. He assured His disciples, "All power is given unto me in heaven and in earth" (Matt. 28:18). It is true that our faith is being tested these days, but now is the time for us to claim His promises and His power and to accept the challenge of the great open doors of opportunity for us. To the Church of Philadelphia, in Asia Minor, Jesus said, "I have set before thee an open door, and no man can shut it" (Rev. 3:8). He is still saying that to the Church today in these final decades of the 20th century.

The Door of Radio

There are, in reality, numerous open doors. First of all, there is the open door of radio. People say, "Russia is closed, Eastern Europe is closed, China is closed, Central Asia is closed, Saudia Arabia is closed," and so on. But the truth is that the doors to these countries are only partially closed. The door of radio is still wide open for the Word of God to go even into these areas. God has set before us in our day an open door that no human hand can shut—the door of radio broadcasting.

People in Russia are hearing the message of Christ today. People in China are hearing that message. People in Eastern Europe are hearing it, and so are those in the Arab countries. This is true

68

of all places of which it is said, "The doors are closed." No generation of Christians ever faced as great an open door as God has unlocked for us in this time and generation. Why must we be so slow to enter this great open door of radio?

According to the December, 1969, issue of the *ICB Bulletin*, published by International Christian Broadcasters, "There are more than 500 million working radio receivers in the world today. Missionary radio uses over 80 transmitters in about 50 locations to beam more than 5000 hours of programming to these receivers each week. (This is *outside* the U.S.A.) Within the U.S.A. there are over 200 radio stations under Christian management broadcasting the gospel. In addition, there are scores of gospel programs released over hundreds of commercial and government stations worldwide."

By means of powerful facilities such as those of HCJB in Quito, Ecuador; the Far East Broadcasting Company in the Philippines, Okinawa, Korea, the United States and the Seychelles (FEBA); Trans World Radio in Monaco, Bonaire and Swaziland; and several others, the message of Jesus Christ is literally being beamed around the world today in most of this planet's major languages.

By means of radio the gospel message penetrates areas such as Russia and the rest of Eastern Europe, the Muslim countries of the Near East, Africa, Pakistan, India and all of Southeast Asia, China, Cuba and all of Latin America. These are doors which God has opened to the people of our generation for use in proclaiming the gospel throughout the nations of the world, and no man can shut these doors.

By the end of 1970 the Back to the Bible Broadcast was being released daily over nearly 600 radio stations, with more than 3800 half-hour programs being broadcast each week. This program can be heard virtually anywhere on earth!

Back to the Bible's Spanish broadcast, *La Biblia Dice* ("The Bible Says"), was simultaneously being released on nearly 70 stations in Latin America, with about 460 releases per week. Our Portuguese broadcast, *A Biblia Fala* ("The Bible Speaks"), was on 16 stations, with about 50 releases per week. Our French broadcast, *La Voix de l'Evangile* ("The Voice of the Gospel"), was on some 50 stations, with about 80 releases per week. Our Italian broadcast, *Voce Della Bibbia* ("Voice of the Bible") was being released four times each week over the powerful facilities of Trans World Radio in Monte Carlo, Monaco. The new Sinhalese and Tamil broadcasts for Ceylon were also being produced and aired. In addition to these broadcasts produced and released under our own auspices, Back to the Bible assists various missionary organizations in the production and release of gospel broadcasts in more than a score of other languages. And we are only *one* group of evangelical Christians engaged in broadcasting the gospel to the world!

In many countries of the world, privately-owned commercial radio stations are willing to accept Christian broadcasts on a purely commercial basis; some countries allow them to be carried on government facilities; in other parts of the world, gospel broadcasting must rely on a few superpower stations covering wide areas with good signals. With opportunities like these, who would dare to say, "The doors are closed"?

Open Minds and Hearts

There is another open door these days that is especially challenging—the open door of people's minds and hearts in many countries of the world. Sometimes national doors are open so that we can go into a given country, but the people's hearts have not been opened. Their minds and ears are closed to the message of Christ. We cannot accomplish much under these circumstances.

The Bible speaks in a number of places about certain people whose hearts the Lord opened. In Acts 16 we read concerning Lydia in Philippi that she was a woman "whose heart the Lord opened" and that she consequently "attended unto the things which were spoken of Paul" (v. 14). This woman became Europe's first known Christian convert and the first member of the Philippian church.

Of the people of Berea we are told, "These were more noble than those in Thessalonica, in that they received the word with all readiness of mind, and searched the scriptures daily, whether those things were so" (Acts 17:11). To those in Thessalonica who had become Christians, the apostle later wrote: "When ye received the word of God which ye heard of us, ye received it not as the word of men, but as it is in truth, the word of God, which effectually worketh also in you that believe" (I Thess. 2:13).

We are witnessing open doors of this kind today in many countries of the world. God has opened the minds and hearts of many people to listen to the gospel where just a few years ago they were utterly closed to that message. The door of radio has been opened and kept open by the God of creation, but human hearts and minds are opened by the God of redemption through the work of His Holy Spirit. Satan tries to blind men's eyes and close their hearts to the message, but the Holy Spirit is able to open these eyes and hearts, and He is doing it.

In Brazil today, for example, there is an almost universal eagerness and hunger to hear the Word of God. In the land of Colombia, where a few years ago the political doors were closed, not only are they open now but people's hearts are wide open to the message of Jesus Christ, and the numbers of believers has greatly multiplied.

Then there is Indonesia, a largely Muslim country where in previous generations the majority of the people were not eager to hear or to receive the message of Jesus Christ. Now they are listening in multitudes, and thousands are accepting the Saviour. They are actually clamoring for the Word of God in both audible and printed form.

Many today have hearts and ears open for the Word of God, even in Russia, Hungary, Poland, Czechoslovakia, and other countries of Eastern Europe. They are listening by radio in their homes and are reading the Word of God wherever and whenever it is available to them.

This is also true of certain countries in Muslim North Africa. And it is true in Roman Catholic Spain. In many countries the hearts and minds of people are open wider to the gospel than we have ever known them to be. Multitudes are listening to the Word of God, and many are responding. These doors—the doors of hearts and ears and minds—are doors no power of man can effectively shut. "I have set before thee an open door, and no man can shut it" (Rev. 3:8).

The Door of Heaven

A third door open to us today and always is the door of heaven. In the Psalms we are told that the Lord "opened the doors of heaven" to His people (Ps. 78:23).

I am sure that the open door of heaven indicates at least two wonderful things. First, God is looking down upon a dark and needy world. The door of heaven is opened from His side, and He sees humanity's spiritual need. He hears the inward cry of human hearts, and He responds to what He sees and hears by showing His compassion for them. This is exemplified by what we read in the Book of Exodus regarding the people of Israel in Egypt (Ex. 1) and what the Lord Himself said to Moses (3:7). The Lord is still looking through the open door of heaven upon the sin, sorrow, bondage and darkness of this fallen race. He sees men bound by the enslaving chains of sin and hears the sighs and groanings of troubled hearts. He knows the sorrows of sinful humanity, and He is moved with compassion toward men.

The open door of heaven indicates something even closer and more vital to us. It is our open door of access to God. This door of prayer is always open to sincere seekers after God and His power. It is never closed. If men could close all other doors to God's people—and of course they cannot—this door would still remain open. As long as this door to heaven and to God's throne of grace and power remains open to us, we can still participate in the work of reaching men and women around the world with the saving message of Jesus Christ.

Here is the open door to any area of the world, regardless of the actions of men—the open door of prayer. No man can shut this door.

Are we using this door? Are we reaching God through it? Or are we so vain and hypocritical that we decry the "closed doors" in the world today while refusing to make use of this most potent door of all. This is the one which supersedes all others. Shame on us if we fail to use it.

As Christians today we need to have a new, honest confrontation with the present-day open doors of opportunity and challenge. Above all others, we must use the open door of Hebrews 4:14-16—the door of prayer.

Chapter 9

A New Criterion of Values

The word "criterion" means "a standard on which a judgment or decision may be based." A criterion is therefore a rule or measure for distinguishing between the right and the wrong, the true and the false.

A good many years ago I was doing some carpenter work—building a house for my brother-in-law. I had a carpenter's ruler which had a bit of one end trimmed off, making it a trifle short of the full and correct measure. I wasn't aware of this, and as a result I made some rather serious errors in my carpentry, wasting some valuable building materials. Ever since then I find myself examining the ruler when I undertake any such work. And it illustrates a principle: We must examine our criteria before we use them.

Poor Evaluations

As Christians, we need the right criterion or the right standard for our lives and our activities. We must have the right estimation of values. Little children often misjudge values and place improper emphases on things. They use their own little

75

measuring stick of a child's mind, and in their childish conceptions they often regard almost worthless things as being among the most valuable in life. Conversely, they think of valuable things as being of very little worth. It is also true that people who have lost their normal mental faculties usually misjudge and improperly evaluate the worth of certain things. Useless things are given a very high priority in their thinking, and valuable things may be ignored or destroyed.

With regard to the true values of life, Christians often are guilty of this same thing. Immature and unbalanced Christians often calculate the real value of the things of life with the wrong measuring stick. The Lord Jesus Christ held up to the world a new criterion of values which most men, sometimes even Christians, utterly miss.

It is true that in the Old Testament a rather strong emphasis was placed on material prosperity, and this was often used as a gauge to measure divine blessings. God did promise material prosperity to His earthly people in the Old Testament era: As they walked in His ways and obeyed His laws and faithfully served Him, He would bless them with security and prosperity. He would also cause the land to be productive and fruitful and give the people long lives on the earth.

Jesus' Standard of Values

But Jesus held up an entirely new criterion for the true children of God. He gave us a new standard of values. He said, "Lay not up for yourselves treasures upon earth, where moth and rust doth corrupt, and where thieves break through and steal: but lay up for yourselves treasures in heaven" (Matt. 6:19,20). He purposely pointed out that the treasures of earth are subject to corruption and theft, both of which are indications of impermanence, and that someday they would all pass away. Therefore, He exhorted men to lay up treasure in heaven and thus have an inheritance that never fades away. This is a wealth that is permanent.

Jesus taught people not to be anxious about such things as food and clothing and the purely material things of life; nor were they to set their affections strongly on these things. He said, "Your Father knoweth what things ye have need of" (v. 8). He assured them that He would take care of those who are indeed His children and that He would take better care of His own children than He does of the birds. In this connection He pointed out that not one single sparrow falls to the ground without His notice. He will take better care of us than He does of the flowers of the field, because they are here for only a brief time and then are gone.

Jesus climaxed His teaching about these things by saying, "Seek ye first the kingdom of God, and his righteousness; and all these things shall be added unto you" (v. 33). Jesus set up a new criterion of values. The greatest value is not in land, clothing or material possessions but rather in seeking the things of the kingdom of God and trusting Him to care for us in this physical life as well as in eternity.

Jesus once said, "What shall it profit a man, if he shall gain the whole world, and lose his own soul?" (Mark 8:36). On a certain occasion, in teaching the right values of earthly existence, He told a story about a certain man who was very rich. This man was a prosperous farmer, and in this particular year his fields had been exceptionally productive. He got such an abundant crop that he made plans to tear down his barns and build larger ones in which to store his goods. Then he planned to say to himself, "Thou hast much goods laid up for many years; take thine ease, eat, drink, and be merry" (Luke 12:19). But that very night God spoke to the man and said to him, "Thou fool, this night thy soul shall be required of thee: then whose shall those things be, which thou hast provided?" (v. 20). Here again, as throughout His teaching ministry, Jesus had held up a new criterion of values and challenged his followers to put the emphasis upon spiritual things rather than upon material things.

The Early Christians

The believers during the first generations of the Church followed this new criterion. In the second chapter of the Book of the Acts we are told that the early Christians shared all things in common. They actually sold their possessions and goods and divided the proceeds among those who had need. In those early years of the gospel many persons, upon becoming Christians, were forced out of work or their own businesses were boycotted. Often they had great difficulty in making a livelihood. So those who had possessions and property simply sold what they had and brought it to the church, where they shared their possessions with one another.

What would induce people to do such an unusual thing? The answer is that they had lost interest in material things and were primarily concerned about the work and the church of Jesus Christ in this world. They were more concerned about the kingdom of God than they were about temporal things. They were interested in spreading the gospel, in making Christ known and in bringing people out of darkness into the light of Christ's love. Therefore, none of these other things held very much value to them. In their minds and hearts the things of true value were the things of eternity, and they lived in order to be witnesses of Christ and to win men to Him.

In the Book of Hebrews we are told about some people of God who "took joyfully the spoiling of [their] goods, knowing . . . that [they had] in heaven a better and an enduring substance" (10:34). These devoted Christians did not mind the loss of their material possessions. They did not hesitate to sacrifice these things for Christ's sake. They lived for the glory of Christ and to serve Him alone.

Human Examples

From time to time throughout history this same criterion has been followed by certain great men of God. Count Von Zinzendorf, a wealthy German nobleman of the 18th century, ignored his position and his riches and devoted his entire life to the spreading of the gospel and to missionary endeavor. He lived entirely for the purpose of making known the good news of salvation through Jesus Christ.

In more recent times, C. T. Studd—a wealthy Christian businessman, a brilliant scholar and a famous athlete of England—sacrificed his possessions and his exalted position to go out as a missionary, first to China, then to India, and finally to Africa. He served for many years as a pioneer missionary in Africa and ultimately died there in 1931. He could have lived a popular, comfortable and luxurious life. But he gave it all up because he had a higher criterion for life's values—the standard Jesus had set. Therefore, he did not live for fame, for wealth or for position but for the one purpose and goal of making Jesus Christ known to the world for which He had died.

About the turn of the century, William Borden, a very wealthy American, likewise turned his back upon his great fortune to go out as a humble missionary of the cross to the land of China. His desire was to preach the gospel to the millions of Muslims in that great land. But he died in Egypt, where he had stopped enroute to China in order to learn the difficult Arabic language. There his body was buried in a humble grave. Thank God there are some people from time to time who have grasped Christ's criterion of values and who have lived solely and soberly for the things of eternity.

Revival and Revision

We need a revival of this criterion among us as contemporary Christians. Our generation is so smug, so comfortable, so at ease and so surrounded with luxuries that many Christians are completely wedded to these material things. They are so attached to their own prosperous countries and to the things of the world which they love that they have become self-seeking Christians instead of those who seek the will and glory of Jesus Christ. Christians are, by and large, very carnal and very materialistically minded. While this situation exists, the work of God around the world is retarded for lack of personnel and lack of material means.

I recently met a Christian Indian from Mexico. Though this man came from a primitive and pagan tribe in a remote area of Mexico, he had become a very devout Christian and an influential leader in the church in his own tribe. About 8000 Christian Indians were under his instruction, ministry and spiritual guidance. This man had been brought to the United States to attend a missionary convention in one of our southern cities. He spoke daily in that convention through a missionary interpreter, since he knew no English. The man who interpreted for him told us that one evening after the daily sessions in the church were over, this Christian Indian prayed, "Father, I don't understand the Christians in this country. But, Father, I think one of their troubles is that they have too much money."

Think of such a prayer as this coming from a man who not many years before had been an unreached pagan! He recognized that Christians in this country are, while perhaps being largely oblivious to the fact, holding up the wrong criterion of values. The primitive Indian saw that they had their hearts set on money and on the material things of this earthly life more than on the things of Christ.

If the world is to be evangelized, we must face the fact here and now that, as Christians, we need to get back to the standards set by Christ and to His criterion of life's values. We must recognize that possessing the things of earth and the present world is not to be our goal. We need to be made willing to surrender our all to Him—our possessions and every part of our lives—and say, "Lord, here I am, and here is what I have. Take what you want, and send me wherever you wish. I am ready to do your will."

Part 2

Missions Dividends

Chapter 10

God's Stock Market

On the stock market everybody knows that *unless you invest* you do not get dividends. It is so on God's market as well. Most certainly it is true of missions.

A young lady, leaving a missionary meeting in company with an older woman, exclaimed to the other rather peevishly, "I just can't get interested in missions." The response of the older woman was, "I am not surprised to hear you say that, Dear. It isn't to be expected that you should be interested. You know, missions are like an investment. It is just like getting interest from the bank—you have to put in a little something; but the more you put in, the more interest you get. The secret of getting more out of missions is to put more in. Time or money or prayer—it does not matter what, but something you yourself put in. Otherwise, you will never have any interest. Try it. Just put a little something into missions and you will be sure of the interest."

The experience of the younger woman is not uncommon, and the counsel of the older one is utterly true. Many cases could be cited of adult Christians' suddenly becoming vitally interested in missions when one or more of their children go to the mission field. They now have an investment in foreign work, and their interest immediately mounts. Cases could also be cited where Christian men who had previously been rather indifferent were suddenly confronted with a challenge to invest a sum of money in missions. The results were the same. Interest mounted. Others, who have been able to contribute neither flesh and blood nor money, have undertaken a ministry of prayer for missionaries. Again, the same results.

Jesus said, "Lay not up for yourselves treasures upon earth, where moth and rust doth corrupt, and where thieves break through and steal: but lay up for yourselves treasures in heaven, where neither moth nor rust doth corrupt, and where thieves do not break through nor steal: for where your treasure is, there will your heart be also. . . . But seek ye first the kingdom of God, and his righteousness; and all these things [the necessities of life] shall be added unto you" (Matt. 6:19-21,33).

Usually at the beginning of a new calendar year or a new fiscal year businessmen and investors meticulously evaluate their stocks and holdings to ascertain as nearly as possible what return they may expect from a given investment. At such times they carefully study the stock market and evaluate their own holdings. Consideration is given to any possible revision of investments, and expert advice is usually sought.

Christians likewise ought to periodically appraise their lives and investments in the light of spiritual standards. Each one should take careful inventory of his entire life—his interests, his activities, his desires and his plans. Where do we stand in relation to the heavenly treasury Jesus talked about? How do our "investments" stand up in the light of His exhortation to men not to lay up treasures on earth where they can be so quickly lost or corrupted? Where do *you* stand at the present time in relation to the heavenly treasury? What have you invested in the bank of heaven? What interest do you have in the work of God throughout the world? What is your interest and investment in overseas missionary work? What dividends have you been getting out of your investment of work, time and money thus far? Are you satisfied, or is your "stock" down? What do you anticipate for the future?

Myra B. Wing, a woman who had invested 40 years of her life in the service of God as a missionary to India, delivered a message entitled "Investments and Dividends," which appeared in the September 3, 1969, issue of *The Alliance Witness*. The essence of the message was that the foreign missionary enterprise is a good investment for the Christian, with respect to both his life and his possessions.

Among other things, Miss Wing stated: "The work of foreign missions offers an attractive field for investment. The corporation is steady and will not liquidate, as sometimes the most stable finance corporation does. Security is guaranteed regardless of the stock market fluctuation. There is no danger of collapse, depression or bank failures, for this investment is backed by the promises of God.

"What profits and dividends can be compared with those which come from investments for God? No business corporation in the world gives such a high rate of interest on any investment. Bankers or stockbrokers could not even attempt to match the dividends. . . . He [God] will guarantee you dividends for eternity."

A Historical Illustration

Meyer Amschel Rothschild, the founder of the famous House of Rothschild banking corporation in Europe and in his day one of the wealthiest men in the world, began his life in a cramped Jewish ghetto in the city of Frankfurt, Germany, in 1743. His parents did not even have a family name. In those times Jews often used signs to mark their houses, and since this family lived in a house identified by a red shield (*rot schild*), the young man took that as his family name.

When Rothschild started out in his business he had some tremendous ideas but no money. He borrowed a small sum from a friend to help him start in business. At that time he had no security to give, and his friend helped him only on the ground of his need, never expecting any return. Years later, when the name of the Rothschild family and firm became internationally famous, the early benefactor received a letter from the House of Rothschild in Frankfurt summoning him to the bank for an important interview. He was now an old man, whose health was broken, whose fortune was gone, and whose family was dependent on him. Missionary-author Wing wrote: "As he entered the private office of the great banker, he was greeted with an unexpectedly warm welcome from the man he had befriended long years earlier. After the old acquaintance had been renewed, Mr.

Rothschild went to his desk and took out a draft for several hundred thousand dollars, handed it to his old friend and said, 'I have sent for you today to pay you the dividends of the stock you entrusted to me nearly 50 years ago.'

"Astounded, the friend refused to take the money, saying he had no claim on it and could not take such a gift. 'It is not a gift' said the banker. 'It is simply the actual profit on the money you loaned me, wisely turned over a great many times until it has accumulated this compound interest.' "

This fittingly illustrates what takes place in the matter of our relationship to God and our investments in His heavenly treasury. Someday Jesus will come again. He will take us to Himself, and we shall then stand before Him to be judged and rewarded for the deeds done for Him in our bodies. Just as Mr. Rothschild gave back to his friend not only the amount of money that had been loaned but also the compound interest on the use of it for more than 50 years, so will our Lord do for us. God, too, has a great business. Not only are the cattle on a thousand hills His property, but the entire universe is His. Everything a Christian invests in His stock will be paid back with compound interest—interest, as our Lord promised, "pressed down, and shaken together, and running over" (Luke 6:38). No business in the world pays the kind of dividends that God pays to His servants.

Miss Wing stated: "There is full proof on every side that missions pays. The missionary enterprise is a success, a world-sweeping success. The gospel works. The business succeeds. It yields dividends beyond reckoning. Missions is bound to be a success, for we are dealing with the work of God."

Are you an investor in God's stock market? Are you an investor in missionary enterprise? Do you have any kind of investment in the work of God? Or are all of your investments and treasures in this world?

A Striking Case

A little boy brought a penny to a lady who was packing a missionary box for India. Because of the little lad's sincerity and desire, she bought a tract with the penny and tucked it into the box. In faraway India this tract was given to a village chief, and it led him to Jesus Christ. He in turn witnessed to his friends. Many of them believed also, and one after another threw away his idols. A church was soon built in that village. A missionary was later sent there to minister, and 1500 persons were ultimately converted to Christ. The gospel is still prospering there. All these wonderful changes resulted from a little boy who invested a penny for God—a glorious example of the dividends God pays for even a very small investment. A little boy gave a penny and the result was a church in the land of India.

Missionary investments pay. The missionary enterprise is a success because it is a divine enterprise under the mandate of Jesus Christ. The preaching of His gospel is attended by the power of God, providing salvation to everyone who believes. The business of world evangelization is a high-paying enterprise; it yields dividends beyond our ability to comprehend or reckon. The Spirit of

God is our partner, the power of God is behind us, the promises of God are all around us, and therefore the work must be fruitful.

A Little Lady, a Big Reward

A few years ago a tiny, aged Negro woman in Texas, Mrs. Josephine Carmichael, gave the savings of her lifetime—a sum of $15,000—toward the erection of an evangelical Christian hospital in Liberia. The president of Liberia was so impressed by what this little woman had done that he decreed she was to be honored with the highest honor his government bestows. The Liberian ambassador to the United States was commissioned to go from Washington, D.C., to the hometown of this little-known saint in Texas, and in the local school auditorium he publicly rewarded her with the highest honor of the Liberian government. He made her a Knight of the Humane Order of African Redemption.

This little woman had indeed cast her bread upon the waters—the hard-earned savings of a lifetime. She did this in order that the people of her own race in distant Liberia might find healing for both their bodies and their souls. The honors she has received in this present life are only a pittance compared to the glorious reward that awaits her in heaven. Even though our Lord often pays great dividends in this life for serving Him, the greatest part of our reward is reserved for us in heaven. Remember the words of Jesus: "Lay up for yourselves treasures in heaven, where neither moth nor rust doth corrupt, and where thieves do not break through nor steal" (Matt. 6:20).

An Oklahoma Businessman

One more example of a person who testified to receiving big dividends on mission investments is a resident of the state of Oklahoma. This man, too, had heeded the exhortation of God's Word, "Cast thy bread upon the waters: for thou shalt find it after many days" (Eccles. 11:1). (Casting bread upon the waters refers to the ancient custom in Bible times of casting wheat, or any seed grain, on the waters of an overflowing river, particularly the river Nile. As the waters receded, the grain, the source of bread, was drawn into the soil, where it ultimately brought a rich harvest.)

A few years ago I was in a missionary conference in the city in Oklahoma where this man was living. He took me out to lunch after the morning church service and told me his story.

Some 25 years earlier, God had spoken to his heart about providing the support for two missionaries who were going out to a primitive Indian tribe in Mexico. He did not have the money available to do this, but God had laid the matter so strongly upon his heart that he went to the bank and borrowed enough money to support the two for one year. He recounted to me that God had so miraculously provided funds that he was able to pay back the loan he had received from the bank, hardly realizing where the money had come from. He continued supporting missionaries from that time forward and was richly blessed by God through doing this.

Shortly after his first experience of supporting the two missionaries in Mexico, he and four other men pooled $300 apiece and formed a small construction company. At the time, he promised the Lord that any gain He granted to him from the new company would be turned directly to the support of foreign missionary work. Sitting across the lunch table that day, his face beaming, he said to me, "Brother, in these past 25 years I have been able, under God, to channel multiplied thousands of dollars to missionary work from that company. God allowed our company to become one of the largest of its kind in the entire state." But that wasn't the whole story. He added, "Because I am now getting a bit too old to shoulder that much responsibility along with my full-time occupation, last year I sold my share of the business. This netted me $300,000. For ever dollar I invested in the business, the profits from which went into missions, God gave me back $1000!"

How is that for dividends? Can any investment company beat God? That $300,000, by the way, also went into missions! This man did not tell me his story to brag or to boast but simply to confirm what I had preached about that very morning—that if we give to God, He will repay us according to the promise of His Son, "good measure, pressed down, and shaken together, and running over" (Luke 6:38).

Christian friend, we can never beat God at the game of investments. Anything we invest for Him in His world cause—possessions, talent, or life itself—He will pay back to us, not just a hundredfold, but a thousandfold or more. Such are the dividends of missions.

Chapter 11

Loaves and Fish

Jesus exhorted every believer to invest in the treasury of heaven, where our investments cannot deteriorate or be taken away from us. But in spite of His exhortation and promise, it seems that comparatively few Christian people give significant heed to what our Lord said. Do we not really believe Jesus' words? Are we hesitant to really trust God? Why are we so anxious to lay up treasures on earth and to trust in these material treasures, the arm of the flesh in the material world, rather than to obey and trust God.

What does the Word of God say about the divine dividends coming to those who invest in God's work, concerning which I have given some current illustrations? There are a number of examples in the Scriptures of various individuals who made certain investments in the work of God and who drew from them great heavenly dividends.

Let us consider the case of the lad who had five loaves of barley bread and two small fish. He gave these to Jesus Christ, and with them our Lord fed a multitude of hungry people numbering 5000 men, plus women and children.

In John 6 we read the statement of Andrew, one of Jesus' disciples: "There is a lad here, which hath five barley loaves, and two small fishes" (v. 9). But then Andrew immediately raised the question that was on the minds of them all: "But what are they among so many?" In view of that great throng of hungry people, what indeed could be done with five loaves of barley bread and two small fish?

But in Matthew, concerning the same incident, we read the words of Jesus: "Bring them hither to me" (14:18). He clearly commanded that the five loaves and the two little fish which the boy had be brought to Him. Taking the lad's loaves and fish, Jesus first gave thanks to the Heavenly Father and then distributed them to the disciples. The disciples gave them to the people, who were seated on the ground. The amazing result was that everyone was filled, and twelve basketsful of fragments were gathered. There are some wonderful lessons for us in this story.

An Existing Need

First of all, note the fact that a great need existed. There were more than 5000 hungry people gathered to listen to Jesus, and they had not eaten all day. Among them were many who were sick. The majority of them were bewildered and confused, "as sheep having no shepherd" (9:36), heartsick and weary both in body and in mind. Worst of all, this was a barren desert area where no food was available (v. 15).

The miracle that Jesus wrought was really performed as an illustration of the truth He wanted

95

to get across to the people: "I am the living bread which came down from heaven: if any man eat of this bread, he shall live for ever" (6:51). He reminded them that Moses had fed their forefathers with miracle bread from heaven every day for 40 years in the wilderness, yet all who ate that bread finally died. In contrast, He was saying in essence, "I am the Living Bread that came down from heaven to give eternal life to men." He actually wrought the miracle in order to teach a lesson.

The multitude of hungry, sick and bewildered people Jesus faced that day is symbolic of a great many in our world today. These people are hungering for the Bread of Life. Masses of men and women who have never been fed spiritually are hungering for eternal life, even though they may not realize it. As Christians today, we stand face to face with the urgent needs of multitudes of men and women who have never tasted the Bread of Life and who are bewildered and frustrated with life. Like Jesus' disciples, we stand today before the tremendous needs of the world, and like them, we are apparently helpless to meet those needs. Referring to the loaves and fish, the disciples were constrained to ask, "What are they among so many?" (6:9). Sometimes it seems that our resources are hopelessly inadequate when measured alongside the great needs. We become discouraged, thinking that there is no possible way we can give the Living Bread to the unfed multitudes of the world.

Think of the situation which the disciples faced. There were perhaps 15,000 or 20,000 hungry people before them, and they had no means to feed them! Naturally there were questions: How can these people be fed? Where shall we secure bread? Where will we find sustenance for them? What can we do? Then one of them said, "There is a lad here, which hath five barley loaves, and two small fishes" (6:9). Only five loaves of bread for so many people! And they were barley loaves at that, the least palatable and the least desired of all bread, eaten only by the very poorest of people! (I have eaten barley bread in Mediterranean lands, and I assure you it is not very tasty.)

But the lad submitted what he possessed into the hands of the Lord Jesus. Upon Jesus' words, "Bring them hither to me" (Matt. 14:18), he readily surrendered what he had. Make no mistake—this was not merely his lunch. Such loaves are usually about nine inches in diameter and about two inches thick. Loaves of that size, made of heavy barley, would probably weigh two pounds or more each. No boy would possibly be carrying five of them around for his lunch. I have already stated that barley bread was eaten by the poorest people. Probably this lad's mother was a poverty-stricken widow, and she likely had sent him to where the crowd was to sell those loaves of barley bread to the hungry people in order that the family might have a little income. The sacrifice he made represented not merely a lunch but probably the total living for his entire family for several days. Yet when Jesus said, "Bring them hither to me," the boy readily surrendered his loaves. That was *his* investment, given into the hands of the Lord in behalf of the hungry multitude.

Dividends!

What did that investment do? We are told in the Bible that all the people ate of the loaves and the fish and were filled (John 6:12). So miraculously did Jesus multiply the boy's contribution that every person in the crowd ate all he desired. Not one went away hungry. Think of the deep-rooted satisfaction in the heart of that little lad to know that Jesus had used his investment to feed all those hungry, needy people! Think, too, of the thrill he must have had in going back home and reciting the story to his family. It must have been a time of great gladness and amazement to them all. *Their* bread and *their* fish, from *their* poor home, were what Jesus Christ used to feed the great multitude of hungry people! That alone was a rather big dividend, was it not?

Then, too, the people knew that it was from the hands of the boy that the bread had come which Jesus had multiplied to satisfy their hunger. Many of them must have looked upon the boy with deep gratitude and appreciation, knowing that he had obeyed the Lord and sacrificed his bread and fish for their sakes. That, too, was a rewarding dividend.

But that was not all. Jesus told the disciples to gather up the fragments that remained in order that nothing should be lost, and they gathered up 12 basketsful of bread. What became of that bread? The Bible does not tell us, but I personally have no doubt that the boy was given all he could carry when he started back home. I suppose the balance probably went to the disciples.

This was indeed a good investment. The boy's investment paid big dividends—dividends that touched not only him but multitudes of others. Anything you and I invest by placing it in the hands of our Saviour in order that His gospel might be given to the hungry multitudes of the world will likewise be a good investment. We will get big dividends here and now, and there will be an abundant treasure laid up for us in heaven.

Chapter 12

Boats and Nets

Let us consider another Bible example of a good "investment." We read in Matthew 4: "Jesus, walking by the sea of Galilee, saw two brethren, Simon called Peter, and Andrew his brother, casting a net into the sea: for they were fishers. And he saith unto them, Follow me, and I will make you fishers of men. And they straightway left their nets, and followed him. And going on from thence, he saw other two brethren, James the son of Zebedee, and John his brother, in a ship with Zebedee their father, mending their nets; and he called them. And they immediately left the ship and their father, and followed him" (vv. 18-22).

In the Gospel of Mark we are similarly told that Jesus was walking by the Sea of Galilee and saw Simon and Andrew cast a net into the sea. He said to them, "Come ye after me, and I will make you to become fishers of men. And straightway they forsook their nets, and followed him" (1:17,18). Note that these men, upon Jesus' call to them to come and follow Him, forsook their boats and their nets. This was a major sacrifice for those men. Possession of a commercial fisherman's outfit, including a boat, was really the fruit of many years' labor. A fishing vessel was not an inexpensive acquisition, and the nets, too, represented a major investment since they had to be large and well made by hand.

For Matthew the publican it meant giving up a job and a career, because he was a tax collector. When Jesus said to him, "Follow me," Matthew left his office and rose to follow Jesus. Those early disciples left all to follow Jesus Christ; they gave up everything. For what purpose? To do what? What did Jesus tell them? "Follow me," He said, "and I will make you fishers of men" (Matt. 4:19). "I will make you to become fishers of men" (Mark 1:17). "From henceforth thou shalt catch men" (Luke 5:10).

These men may not have understood the total import of Jesus' call at the time, but they did understand that He was challenging them to leave all, to give up everything, and to follow Him. This was a real sacrifice for them, an "investment" of all they had for the cause of Christ. They gave up their possessions, their homes and their family ties to obey the Lord's call and His divine commission. In short, they gave up their lives.

They may have wondered at times about the wisdom of their decision, and on one occasion Peter even said, "Behold, we have forsaken all, and followed thee; what shall we have therefore?" (Matt. 19:27). Jesus Christ has called many people to give up families, friends and occupations for His cause, and many have responded. Some have gone out on the deep waters to cast their nets to bring men to Christ, sometimes facing grave dangers. Others have given up their material possessions to support those who have gone. No doubt a good many of these have asked, "What shall we have therefore? Has it been worthwhile? What has been achieved? Have we been wise? Has our life brought gain or loss?"

What were the actual benefits of the sacrifice made by these men in giving up their nets and boats? I would like to cite three dividends they received from their "investment."

First, they had blessed and intimate fellowship with the incarnate Son of God. For three and a half years they walked and talked with Him. They heard His voice, realizing, as the people said, "Never man spake like this man" (John 7:46). They heard Him as He talked in public hour after hour, and then they listened to Him in private as He taught them about the things of God and of heaven. Not only did they hear His voice, they witnessed His power. They saw Him heal the sick, cast out demons, still the storms and raise the dead.

They also experienced that power in themselves. We are told that He gave them power to cast out unclean spirits and to heal all manner of sickness and disease. And they saw His glory. Simon Peter said, "We . . . were eyewitnesses of his majesty. For he received from God the Father honour and glory. . . . We were with him in the holy mount" (II Pet. 1:16-18). And the Apostle John said, "(And we beheld his glory, the glory as of the only begotten of the Father,) full of grace and truth" (John 1:14).

Looking back, would those men at the end of those three and a half years have withdrawn their "investment?" Would they have said, "Let us go back to our boats and nets"? Of course not! They knew that it had been a worthwhile sacrifice.

In the second place, they had the privilege of bringing blessing into the lives of others during those three and a half years. As they were empowered by the Holy Spirit, they set men free from the power of Satan and they delivered people from suffering and disease. What joy they must have experienced in doing this. On one occasion they came back rejoicing because, as they said, "Even the devils are subject unto us through thy name" (Luke 10:17). The ministry of those whom Jesus called influenced many other people to turn to Christ and follow Him, and that was another dividend.

But beyond all of this, think of what their ministry meant in the world after Christ's death and resurrection. When Christ said, "Follow me," He did not mean that they were to give up their boats and nets for only three and a half years; it was to be for the rest of their lives. What happened after His resurrection? On the Day of Pentecost 3000 people were saved. The Church was born and was established in the world. During the following years the gospel went forth throughout the world because of these men. The Church grew and spread. Cities and whole communities were transformed. Countries were turned upside down. Sweeping spiritual victories were won. Paul wrote to the believers in Thessalonica: "For our gospel came not unto you in word only, but also in power, and in the Holy Ghost, and in much assurance" (I Thess. 1:5). Even the New Testament Scriptures were written in part by these men.

These were the dividends that came from their investment of their lives and skills in the cause of Christ. Was it a good investment? Certainly it was! It brought tremendous dividends on earth and even greater rewards in heaven.

Chapter 13

A Man Who Surrendered His Son

The first missionaries Christ called were His 12 disciples. After several months of following Him, they said to Him one day, "Behold, we have forsaken all, and followed thee; what shall we have therefore?" (Matt. 19:27). They were asking, "What are we going to get in return for what we have done? What will be our reward? What dividends will we get for our sacrificial investments?" Jesus answered very quickly, "Every one that hath forsaken houses, or brethren, or sisters, or father, or mother, or wife, or children, or lands, for my name's sake, shall receive an hundredfold, and shall inherit everlasting life" (v. 29).

In the world of finance a ten percent dividend would be considered a pretty fair return on invested money. But the Lord promises 10,000 percent—100 times more than the investment.

Consider with me another example from the Scriptures: Abraham, who gave his son Isaac to the Lord. God's command to Abraham to offer his son in sacrifice was clear, but certainly it was very bewildering to the man. God had told Abraham, when He first called him to leave his native land

and to go into the Promised Land, that He would make of him a great nation and that the nation descending from him would be a channel of blessing to the whole world. God had said, "I will make of thee a great nation. . . . And in thee shall all families of the earth be blessed" (Gen. 12:2,3). "I will make thy seed as the dust of the earth" (13:16). "Look now toward heaven, and tell the stars, if thou be able to number them. . . . So shall thy seed be" (15:5).

But Abraham and Sarah advanced in years until both of them were very old, yet they did not have even one child. They finally doubted God's promise and God's purpose, and upon Sarah's suggestion Abraham begot a son by her maid, Hagar. This act of faithlessness caused all of them serious trouble and heartache. In due time, however, Isaac was miraculously born, according to the promise and purpose of God.

"It came to pass after these things, that God did tempt Abraham, and said unto him, Abraham: and he said, Behold, here I am. And he said, Take now thy son, thine only son Isaac, whom thou lovest, and get thee into the land of Moriah; and offer him there for a burnt-offering upon one of the mountains which I will tell thee of. And Abraham rose up early in the morning, and saddled his ass, and took two of his young men with him, and Isaac his son, and clave the wood for the burnt-offering, and rose up, and went unto the place of which God had told him. . . . And they came to the place which God had told him of; and Abraham built an altar there, and laid the wood in order, and bound Isaac his son, and laid him on the altar upon the wood. And Abraham stretched forth his hand, and took the knife to slay his son. And the angel of the Lord called unto him out of heaven, and said, Abraham, Abraham: and he said, Here am I. And he said, Lay not thine hand upon the lad, neither do thou any thing unto him: for now I know that thou fearest God, seeing thou hast not withheld thy son, thine only son from me" (Gen. 22:1-3,9-12).

When Isaac was a young man, probably in his late teens or early twenties, a strange and hard command came to Abraham from God: he was to offer his son in sacrifice upon an altar. Strange indeed it was that God should give such a drastic order as this. Why would He want a man to offer his own son as a burnt offering, especially Abraham's son Isaac. Abraham loved his promised son dearly, for he was to be the heir and the channel of all the divine promises. But by this time in Abraham's experience he had become strong in faith, believing that God was able to raise Isaac even from the dead. So we read in Genesis 22 that Abraham rose early in the morning, saddled his ass, took Isaac his son, and went to the place of which God had told him. How perplexed and bewildered Abraham's mind and heart must have been as he traveled toward Mount Moriah! We read the story casually, not realizing how hard it must have been for him. But try to think of what it meant to him to make such an investment in obedience to the command of God—to offer his own son, the son in whom he had placed all his hopes and in whom all the divine promises centered. God's divine purpose in and through Isaac had been expressed to Abraham several times. But that same God told him to go up a mountain and offer this young man in sacrifice. Abraham's mind must have been greatly bewildered and his heart and soul torn asunder.

One can only vaguely imagine how filled with sorrow his soul must have been that day as he journeyed toward Moriah and how heavy his heart must have been. But Abraham obeyed. He did exactly what God commanded him to do. He was willing to invest his own beloved son, the one in whom the whole future seemed centered, in response to the word and command of God. He went to Moriah, erected the altar, and was beginning the very act of slaying his son when God suddenly spoke. "Abraham," he heard God say, "I never intended you to slay your son. I only wanted to find out if you had now learned to believe Me and trust Me and were willing to obey Me no matter what the cost. I wanted to find out if you were willing to give up anything you had for My sake." That was the climax of the Mount Moriah episode.

What were the dividends of Abraham's obedience and investment? First of all, he got Isaac back, like a son who had been raised from the dead. Furthermore, he received a glorious commendation from God Himself: "Now I know that thou fearest God, seeing thou hast not withheld thy son, thine only son from me" (v. 12). What a commendation this was, from the lips of God Himself! In the Book of Hebrews Abraham is mentioned among the great heroes of faith, and in the Book of Romans he is held up as the great example of faith and the father of faith. What dividends are these!

Not only did Abraham get Isaac back, and not only did he have the commendation of God, but as a further result God's great, divine purpose through Abraham and Isaac was reaffirmed and ultimately carried out. "By myself have I sworn, saith the Lord, for because thou hast done this thing, and hast not withheld thy son, thine only son: that in blessing I will bless thee, and in multiplying I will multiply thy seed as the stars of the heaven, and as the sand which is upon the sea shore; and thy seed shall possess the gate of his enemies; and in thy seed shall all the nations of the earth be blessed; because thou hast obeyed my voice" (Gen. 22:16-18).

Through the children of Abraham God gave to the world the written revelation of Himself. It was through the seed of Abraham that the knowledge of God was preserved among men; without him all of mankind would have become totally pagan. It was through the children of Abraham that salvation was brought into the world, for through the Jews, God's divine plan of redemption was brought to fruition and actuality. This is what He meant when He said to Abraham, "In thy seed shall all the families of the earth be blessed" (v. 18). Through that seed, or that nation, Christ the Saviour came into the world. It was through the seed of Abraham that the Church was originally established in this world, for the very first followers of Christ after His death—people who were called "Christians"—were actually Jewish by birth and by former belief.

Ah yes, these were big dividends from the divine investment Abraham was willing to make.

God has called for many a son and daughter to be offered to Himself on the altar of missionary service. Sometimes parents have had battles over this, just as Abraham doubtless had as he journeyed toward Moriah. When they knew that God was asking their son or their daughter to give up all cherished plans and to sacrifice so many things that life holds dear in order to go and bury himself or herself in some distant foreign field, it was to them like a cruel altar of service and sacrifice. Parents have battled this, some have been bewildered over it, and some have rebelled. But others have said Yes. And how rich have been the dividends that have come to those who did say to God, "Yes, Lord, I will obey You. I give You all that I have and all that I am. I am willing to give up anything to heed Your call and to fulfill Your purpose." It has been through those lives, who, like Isaac, have been surrendered to God on the altar of service and sacrifice, that the peoples of the world have received untold blessings. The blessing of God came to the world through Isaac, but it was because of Abraham's obedience and surrender that it was so.

Part 3

The Christian's Divine
Commission

Chapter 14

Like Mandate

"Then the same day at evening, being the first day of the week, when the doors were shut where the disciples were assembled for fear of the Jews, came Jesus and stood in the midst, and saith unto them, Peace be unto you. And when he had so said, he showed unto them his hands and his side. Then were the disciples glad, when they saw the Lord. Then said Jesus to them again, Peace be unto you: as my Father hath sent me, even so send I you" (John 20:19-21).

The last part of this statement by Jesus can easily be glossed over, and this is often done. But in reality it is a very profound and important statement from the lips of the risen Christ.

"As my Father hath sent me, even so send I you" (v. 21). This declaration indicates that whatever was required of Jesus in His coming to this earth is also required of us who are His followers. Whatever manner, whatever purpose, whatever sacrifice, whatever motivation, and whatever self-abdication characterized Christ on His mission in the world must characterize us as His servants in this world as well.

These words were addressed to Jesus' disciples corporately, and they therefore apply to all His followers, including Christians today. As it was with Him, the divine Servant of Jehovah, so must it be with us, as His servants. We need to find out just what this means for you and for me.

First of all, when Jesus said, "As my Father hath sent me, even so send I you," He must have meant that we are under a similar divine mandate. "As I came into this world," He was saying, "so I send you into this world." Jesus came into this world as the only begotten Son of God, under the mandate of His Heavenly Father. A "mandate," according to the dictionary, is "an authoritative command; an authorization to act given to a representative." Christ, the eternal Son of God, was sent into this world under the eternal Father's commission and mandate.

It was clearly mandatory for Him to come; He was sent by God. The Scriptures emphasize this. For example, we read in Galatians 4:4: "When the fulness of the time was come, God sent forth his Son, made of a woman, made under the law." The Apostle John wrote: "We have seen and do testify that the Father sent the Son to be the Saviour of the world" (I John 4:14). In John's Gospel we are told, "God sent . . . his Son into the world . . . that the world through him might be saved" (John 3:17).

Jesus was always aware of His task. He knew that He had come into this world under the divine mandate of His Heavenly Father. He made many statements to this effect: "My meat is to do the will of him that sent me, and to finish his work" (4:34); "For I came down from heaven, not to do mine own will, but the will of Him that sent me" (6:38); "My doctrine is not mine, but his that sent me" (7:16); "Ye both know me, and ye know whence I am: and I am not come of myself, but he that sent me is true, whom ye know not. But I know him: for I am from him, and he hath sent me" (vv. 28,29).

Near the close of His ministry Jesus said to His disciples, "Yet a little while am I with you, and then I go unto Him that sent me" (v. 33). To His adversaries He once said, "If God were your Father, ye would love me: for I proceeded forth and came from God; neither came I of myself, but he sent me" (8:42). He said, "I must work the works of him that sent me, while it is day: the night cometh, when no man can work" (9:4). Jesus knew well that He was in the world under the mandate of His Heavenly Father.

This heavenly mandate indicated sovereignty on the part of the Sender, who was God the Father. A father possesses sovereignty over his son, not vice versa. This is true in the Godhead: the eternal Father exercised His sovereignty over the Son and sent Him into our world. This relationship which exists in the Holy Trinity is carried over into the relationships of the human family as well. A father is recognized as the authority over his son. A father has the sovereign right to send and to commission his son wherever he may desire and for whatever purpose he may determine.

"As My Father was sovereign over Me," Jesus was really saying, "so I am sovereign over you. I am your Lord and your Master. I am in authority over you. I am to have preeminence in all things in your life and in your planning." It is essential that

115

Christians recognize and acknowledge the lordship of Jesus Christ in their lives, just as Jesus recognized the lordship of His Heavenly Father over Him. The Bible constantly and consistently speaks of the lordship of Christ, yet all too few Christians seem to recognize His sovereignty and lordship over them. Someone long ago said, "Jesus Christ must be Lord of all, or He is not our Lord at all."

Not only do these words of Jesus imply sovereignty on the part of the Sender, but they imply and demand submission on the part of the One who was sent. When Jesus first came into the world, and even before He came into the world, He was completely submissive to the will of His Father. He said to the Father, "Sacrifice and offering thou wouldest not, but a body hast thou prepared me. In burnt-offerings and sacrifices for sin thou hast had no pleasure. Then said I, Lo, I come (in the volume of the book it is written of me,) to do thy will, O God" (Heb. 10:5-7). Before He came into this world, Jesus knew that a holy God could not accept the sacrifice of mere animals for the sins of a human soul and that He had prepared for His Son a human body in which He was to live and suffer and die in order to make atonement for mankind's sins. And in submission to His Father's desire He exclaimed, "I come . . . to do thy will, O God." Yet when He said this, He must have known all that would be demanded of Him in the flesh. Still, before He ever came into the world, He was fully submitted to His Father.

Throughout the time Jesus was in the world He was in continual submission to the Father's will. He repeatedly made statements like this: "I seek not mine own will, but the will of the Father which hath sent me" (John 5:30); "He that sent me is with me: the Father hath not left me alone; for I do always those things that please him" (8:29). Just before He went to the cross, bowing in deep pain and agony in the darkness of Gethsemane's garden, He still said, "Not my will, but thine, be done" (Luke 22:42). And even standing in Pilate's judgment hall, He was docile and submissive. And finally, in those last moments of His earthly life, He said, "Father, into thy hands I commend my spirit" (Luke 23:46). He was submitted to the will of His Heavenly Father to the very end.

When Jesus said, "As my Father hath sent me, even so send I you" (John 20:21), He meant, "As My Father was sovereign over Me, I am sovereign over you. As I was always submissive to the will of My Father, you must likewise now be submissive to My will. As I was obedient and subject to the plan of My Father for the whole world, so I now send you in submission to My will into the whole world to proclaim repentance and remission of sins in My name among all nations." Just as Jesus was required to be obedient to the mandate of His Father, so are we now required to be obedient to His mandate over us.

His mandate to us is very clear. In the final chapter of Matthew we see Him standing before His disciples and saying, "All power is given unto me in heaven and in earth. Go ye therefore, and teach [make disciples of] all nations, baptizing them in the name of the Father, and of the Son, and of the Holy Ghost: teaching them to observe all things whatsoever I have commanded you"

(28:18-20). Just as He was given a mandate from His Father, He, in turn, has given us a mandate. The Father's mandate was for Him to go and to make atonement for the sins of the world; Christ's mandate to us is that we involve ourselves with world missions. We are to engage in an endeavor of world evangelization, preaching the gospel to every person in all the world.

World evangelization is mandatory. It is not a matter of personal choice but of divine command. The only alternative to involvement in world missions is disobedience to Christ. Jesus said, "As my Father hath sent me [under His authority and under His sovereignty], even so send I you [under My authority and under My sovereignty]" (John 20:21). When a person or a group of persons is given a mandate by someone who is in a position of authority, they can only comply or refuse, obey or disobey, submit or rebel.

Notice the various persons involved in these words of Christ. "My Father" refers to the sovereign, almighty, eternal God. "I" refers to the risen Christ, the Saviour of all who have trusted Him. But who is meant by "you"? Who were addressed and who were included? Did He mean only those few men who were present when He spoke these words? No, He clearly meant all His disciples, all His followers since that day. He means every believer.

Will you be obedient to His mandate, as He was obedient to His Heavenly Father's mandate? This is the question each Christian must face.

Chapter 15

Like Manner

When Jesus said, "As my Father hath sent me, even so send I you" (John 20:21), He meant not only that believers were to go under a *mandate* such as the Father had given Him but also that they were to go in the same *manner* as He had come. But how did Jesus come into the world? What was demanded of Him when He came?

In the beginning, Jesus was with God and was God. He had the very likeness and nature of God Himself. He was the "brightness of [God's] glory, and the express image of his person" (Heb. 1:3), and all the angels of God worshiped Him (v. 6). To leave that position in heaven and to come into this world was a drastic and extremely important step. God the Son revealed God the Father in three specific ways.

First, the Son of God became the Son of Man and took upon Himself human flesh. Thus He identified Himself with those whom He had come to save. "The Word [the eternal *Logos*, which was in the beginning with God] was made flesh, and dwelt among us, (and we beheld his glory, the glory as of the only begotten of the Father,) full of grace and truth" (John 1:14). The Apostle Paul wrote in his epistle to the Romans that He was "made of the seed of David according to the flesh" (Rom. 1:3). We are told that God sent "his own Son in the likeness of sinful flesh," and in so doing, He "condemned sin in the flesh" (8:3). We are also told that He "made himself of no reputation, and took upon him the form of a servant, and was made in the likeness of men" (Phil. 2:7). In a letter to Timothy, the Apostle Paul burst out with this tremendous statement: "Great is the mystery of godliness: God was manifest in the flesh" (I Tim. 3:16).

Christ had to come as a human being in order to make saving contact with humanity. The two great purposes for His coming into this world in the form of humanity were to reveal God to men and to redeem men—make them acceptable in God's sight.

John 1:1,2 declares that Jesus, "the Word," was the eternal expression and revelation of Almighty God. But as such, in the beginning, He was in heaven, and men could not approach Him there. Hence they could not see or grasp the revelation He in His own nature gave of the eternal God. Therefore, Jesus Christ was sent down to earth to bring the revelation of God within the reach and touch of man. He was the incarnated Translation of the divine *Logos* into human language—a language that was perceivable and understandable to men. Jesus Christ has well been called "the Illustrated Edition of the Word of God."

Second, Jesus revealed God to men by verbal declaration. He talked to men about God, His Father, and about His glorious kingdom. He talked to them about His love and concern for mankind. Throughout the Gospels we read what He taught, and the people said of Him, "Never man spake like this man" (John 7:46).

But beyond mere declaration He also revealed God by vivid demonstration. For example, Nicodemus, the Jerusalem rabbi, said, "No man can do these miracles that thou doest, except God be with him" (John 3:2). The people who beheld His miraculous acts said, "We never saw it on this fashion" (Mark 2:12).

Jesus also came to redeem man. When He left heaven He said to God the Father, "Sacrifice and offering thou wouldest not, but a body hast thou prepared me" (Heb. 10:5). The Old Testament sacrifices and offerings could never take away sin. But the Father prepared for His Son a human body, and through the marvel and mystery of that incarnation the Son of God became our Kinsman in order that He might be our Redeemer.

Through this divine incarnation, Jesus entered into complete identification with mankind. "Both he that sanctifieth and they who are sanctified are all of one: for which cause he is not ashamed to call them brethren. . . . Forasmuch then as the children are partakers of flesh and blood, he also himself likewise took part of the same; that through death he might destroy him that had the power of death, that is, the devil. . . . Wherefore in all things it behoved him to be made like unto his brethren, that he might be a merciful and faithful high priest in things pertaining to God, to make reconciliation for the sins of the people" (Heb. 2:11,14,17).

Christ was made one with mankind. He identified fully and unreservedly with humanity. How else could He have won men to Himself? How else could He have become our Kinsman-Redeemer and our sympathetic Priest? He had to taste human humiliation, sorrow, pain, hatred and misunderstanding as well as false accusations, rejections, revilings, temptations, trials and discouragements. He was a "Man of sorrows, and acquainted with grief" (Isa. 53:3). This is the common lot of humanity. He knew what it was to have a broken heart. He identified Himself with humanity, and all of these things are a part of human existence.

Samuel Escobar, a distinguished Latin American Christian leader, stated: "This is the marvelous truth of the Incarnation: God made Himself Man. The Word of God was made flesh and lived among men. Jesus did not fulfill His mission from afar. . . . His redemptive past would not have been possible without this identification, this living as man in the midst of men. Friend of sinners, He accepts them and eats with them. . . . This is the Lord who sends us. And this is *how* He sends us."

Third, Christ revealed God the Father to the human race by His willingness to die as man's substitute. It was necessary for Him to actually die in the place of guilty sinners. He became the substitute for sinners by paying the penalty for human sin. In the words of the Bible, God "hath made him to be sin for us, who knew no sin; that we might be made the righteousness of God in him" (II Cor. 5:21).

Upon leaving heaven to come into this world, He said to the Father, "A body hast thou prepared

122

me" (Heb. 10:5). He knew that in that body He must suffer the guilt and penalty of human sin. As Simon Peter wrote: "Who his own self bare our sins in his own body on the tree" (I Pet. 2:24). The same apostle also stated: "Christ also hath once suffered for sins, the just for the unjust, that he might bring us to God" (3:18). The Prophet Isaiah prophetically said of Him, "Surely he hath borne our griefs, and carried our sorrows: yet we did esteem him stricken, smitten of God, and afflicted. But he was wounded for our transgressions, he was bruised for our iniquities: the chastisement of our peace was upon him; and with his stripes we are healed. All we like sheep have gone astray; we have turned every one to his own way; and the Lord hath laid on him the iniquity of us all" (Isa. 53:4-6).

This is what the "as" meant in Jesus' statement, "As my Father hath sent me, even so send I you" (John 20:21). It meant incarnation—taking upon Himself human flesh. It meant identification with fallen humanity. And it meant becoming the substitute for sinners and taking their guilt. Therefore, His words, "As my Father hath sent me, even so send I you," imply that we must repeat and perpetuate His experience, to the highest degree possible, in our own lives and service. As Christians, our lives in this world are to be, in a certain sense, a perpetuation of the divine incarnation. Not many days before Jesus spoke these words, He had said to those same men, "Abide in me, and I in you" (15:4). Therefore, He was saying in essence, "As I am God in the flesh, so I now send you forth as incarnations of My own divine Self. I shall dwell in you by My Spirit. Go

123

ye, therefore, into all the world and reveal Me to men. Exhibit the grace of God and reveal the truth of God My Father and of Me His Son, whom He sent into the world."

In order for us to truly bring the message of salvation into an understandable contact with humanity, people must see in our own lives the very presence of Jesus Himself. We are to be perpetuations of His incarnated Self. We are to make the gospel known by declaring it from our redeemed lips and by demonstrating it in our redeemed lives.

The missionary must be the visible expression of the truth of Jesus, whom He proclaims. Señor Escobar further said, "Sent by Him, we are also men in the midst of men. We live in a specific society, subject to human laws and to the contingencies . . . to which all our earthly fellowmen are subject."

John R. W. Stott, of England, commenting on the words of our basic text, said, "While these words represent the simplest form of the Great Commission, they express the most profound truth. . . . In these words Jesus gave us not only a command to evangelize but also a model for evangelization. The Church's mission in the world is to be like Christ in every way." This same preacher and writer also said, "Our failure to obey the implications of the mandate, 'So send I you,' constitutes the most tragic weakness of evangelical Christians. . . . We do not identify ourselves with [unbelievers]. We believe so strongly in proclamation that we tend to proclaim our message at a distance. . . . We appear to be giving advice from the security of the shore to men who are drowning. We do not dive in to help them. We are frightened at the thought of getting wet, and besides, this implies many dangers. We forget that Jesus did not send His salvation from heaven; He visited us in our humanity."

The missionary must identify himself with people the way Jesus came into this world and identified Himself with us all. Have we forgotten this? Have we merely tried to preach the gospel *at* people? Have we been trying to tell them "from afar"? This will not work. We must come close to them. Just as Jesus could not fulfill His divine mission in this world from afar, neither can we. We must get close to people. We must learn their language. We must learn their way of life. We must learn their pattern of thought. We must identify ourselves with them in their needs. Otherwise they will neither hear nor understand our message.

At the Latin American Evangelical Congress in Bogotá, Colombia, in 1969, one of the South American speakers asserted that the task of the Church does not end in mere proclamation, essential as that is. He said, "The Church is more than an able proclaimer of ... intellectual precepts; it is the visible expression of the truth it proclaims. . . . It is evident how artificial it is to teach techniques on how to communicate the message apart from a primary emphasis on the Christian life and a united testimony to the Christian community."

In a certain very real sense, we must also carry on Christ's very work of substitution. This is not easy and cannot be done in mere human strength, but it is what we must do in order to fulfill our divine commission. Jesus came to bear in His own

125

body the guilt, the burden and the fruits of human sin. He became our Substitute. And in a certain real sense, we must likewise bear upon our hearts and in our lives the burden and the blight of fallen humanity. Someone has said, "True missionaries must have true sensitivity to human need." Missionaries who go out to other countries must actually bear and share the sorrows of the people in their own souls. They must suffer with those people. They must identify with them in their need and in their suffering and misery. In a genuine sense we must even identify with people's guilt and poverty of soul, just as Jesus came into this world to identify Himself with our guilt and spiritual poverty.

Can we vicariously take on ourselves the guilt of men's sins? Look at some of the men of God in the Bible who apparently did this very thing. When Nehemiah prayed for his people, who had returned to their own land after the exile, he prayed as if the guilt of his people were his own guilt. He cried out, "O Lord God, . . . I . . . confess the sins of the children of Israel, which we have sinned against thee: both I and my father's house have sinned" (Neh. 1:5,6). Ezra prayed exactly the same way, "O my God, I am ashamed . . . : for our iniquities are increased" (Ezra 9:6). Likewise Daniel, who prayed, "We have sinned, and have committed iniquity, and have done wickedly, and have rebelled, . . . Therefore the curse is poured upon us, and the oath that is written in the law of Moses the servant of God, because we have sinned against him" (Dan. 9:5,11). Daniel confessed the sins of his people as his very own transgressions, yet he himself was a righteous man and above reproach

126

before God. When these men prayed, it was as though they were taking the place of substitution in paying for the sins and guilt of their people. How can we understand people unless we somehow identify ourselves with them in their fallen sinful state? And how can we get a responsive ear and heart from them?

In my home city there is a rescue mission which is superintended by a converted alcoholic. This man has a unique opportunity to help victims of alcoholism, for he knows what alcoholism is. He can, through firsthand knowledge, understand the men he is trying to help and win them to the Lord Jesus. Because he is able to identify with them he is able to convey the message of the gospel to them in a way that no one else could.

When Jesus said, "As my Father hath sent me, even so send I you," He meant, "As I became incarnated and identified with you, so you are now to be replicas of that incarnation, and you are to identify yourselves with the fallen people of the world. You are to bear their burdens, their sorrows and even their guilt upon your own souls." When we do this, people will understand our message and they will respond.

It is altogether likely that when Jesus spoke these words to the disciples, they did not fully understand the import of what He was saying. But they learned later what He meant. They learned that to go into the world as Jesus had come into the world meant that they would be hated, rejected, persecuted, and punished; they would suffer all kinds of perils and poverty—even death. But because Jesus said, "As my Father hath sent me, even so send I you," they faithfully carried out that mission.

Are we ready to accept this divine commission? Are we willing to accept this assignment as ours? It is the only way the people of the world can be brought to know the Saviour. As He came, so we must go.

Chapter 16

Like Mission

Jesus told His disciples, "As my Father hath sent me, even so send I you" (John 20:21). That believers are to go forth under like mandate and in like manner has been discussed. They are also to go on like mission. In effect Jesus was saying, "My Father sent me into this world on a divine mission, and now I send you to perform the mission My Father sent Me to begin."

But what was Jesus' mission in the world? Why was He sent? What was His Father's reason and purpose in sending Him? If we are to understand our own Christian mission in the world, we must perceive the nature of His mission.

A careful study of the Scriptures indicates that Jesus' earthly mission was threefold. First, He came into this world to reveal God to man. The knowledge of God had all but perished from the earth by the time Jesus appeared, and the world into which He came was a very dark one. As the Apostle Paul showed, the people of the pagan, Gentile world had refused to retain God in their knowledge. They deliberately and willfully shut Him out of their thinking, and therefore God had given them over to reprobation, spiritual darkness

129

and moral degradation. The world into which Jesus came was, for the most part, in heathen darkness. Even in the chosen nation of Israel the divine light was shining but dimly, so that Jesus was compelled to say to the leaders of His own nation, "Ye neither know me, nor my Father: if ye had known me, ye should have known my Father also" (John 8:19). God had been revealed to them in marvelous ways, yet at the time of Christ they did not really know God. Jesus called them "blind leaders of the blind" (Matt. 15:14). The Apostle Paul went so far as to say that the name of God was blasphemed in the heathen world through them (Rom. 2:24).

Jesus came into that dark world to bring divine light from heaven—light to lighten every man coming into the world. While He was in the world, He plainly said, "I am the light of the world" (John 8:12). His mission was that of divine revelation.

Second, Jesus came not only to reveal God but also to redeem men. This was the ultimate objective, the primary purpose for His being sent into this world by the Father. His mission of revealing God was for the express purpose of being able to bring men to God. If He had not come on a mission of redemption, there would have been no point in revealing God to men, for what would be the value in men knowing about God if they could not be reconciled to Him?

Third, Jesus came to rear His Church. During the time His disciples were with Him for instruction and training, He said to them, "I will build my church; and the gates of hell [hades] shall not prevail against it" (Matt. 16:18). He was sent into the world by the Father to take out of the nations a people for His name—a redeemed people, the Church. Like the merchant of His own parable, He came into the world to seek out and purchase the "pearl of great price" (Matt. 13:46). He bought the pearl at the price of His own blood in order that He might claim His precious pearl, which is the Church.

It is the second aspect of His divine mission that I wish to emphasize here—the fact that He came to redeem man. The Scriptures plainly state this aspect of His mission: "He hath visited and redeemed his people. . . . To give knowledge of salvation unto his people by the remission of their sins, through the tender mercy of our God; whereby the dayspring from on high hath visited us" (Luke 1:68,77,78). "Christ hath redeemed us from the curse of the law, being made a curse for us" (Gal. 3:13). "When the fulness of the time was come, God sent forth his Son, made of a woman, made under the law, to redeem them that were under the law" (4:4). "Our Saviour Jesus Christ . . . gave himself for us, that he might redeem us from all iniquity, and purify unto himself a peculiar people" (Titus 2:13,14). "By his own blood [Christ] entered in once into the holy place, having obtained eternal redemption for us" (Heb. 9:12). And concerning His own mission, Jesus said, "The Son of man came not to be ministered unto, but to minister, and to give his life a ransom for many" (Mark 10:45).

Christ's mission—to seek the lost—is described in various ways in the Scriptures. There is a very striking and doubtless prophetic statement in Psalm 130: "With him is plenteous redemption" (v. 7). "Plenteous" redemption refers to abundant,

131

full and complete redemption, fully matching and meeting all the complex needs of mankind. God's provision of redemption for man, as seen in the Scriptures and in the light of human need, is a multiple and complex transaction, or divine operation.

In straightforward, simple language Jesus said, "The Son of man is come to seek and to save that which was lost" (Luke 19:10). In one of His parables He compared mankind to lost sheep, sheep who have gone astray. Each has gone his own willful way, and the Great Shepherd comes seeking these lost sheep, laying them on His own shoulders, and bringing them back to the Father's fold.

Jesus specifically referred to two groups of lost sheep among men. "The lost sheep of the house of Israel" (Matt. 15:24) were those of His own nation and people. "Other sheep . . . which are not of this fold" (John 10:16) were not of the nation of Israel. These were Gentiles. He went on to say, "Them also I must bring, . . . and there shall be one fold, and one shepherd" (v. 16). In that same context He declared, "I am the good shepherd: the good shepherd giveth his life for the sheep. . . . As the Father knoweth me, even so know I the Father: and I lay down my life for the sheep. . . . And I give unto them eternal life; and they shall never perish, neither shall any man pluck them out of my hand" (vv. 11,15,28).

When Jesus said to His disciples, "As my Father hath sent me, even so send I you" (20:21), He was saying that their mission must be to go to the lost sheep of humanity scattered over the face of the earth and point them to Christ. There are still multitudes who are like sheep without a

132

shepherd, and we must seek them and bring them to His fold.

What about the multitudes who are still scattered over the earth and have never even heard the mention of His name? What about those who are far from the fold and who have never heard the voice of the Shepherd? Is it not clearly our mission to seek these people?

Jesus' divine mission of redemption involved bringing to men a full and personal knowledge of God and placing them into a living relationship with Him. In His prayer to His Father, recorded in John 17, He said, "This is life eternal, that they might know thee the only true God, and Jesus Christ, whom thou hast sent" (v. 3). These words constitute a definition of eternal life and direction concerning how to find it. Men must come into a personal knowledge of the one and only true God, and they must come into a relationship with Him through Jesus Christ, whom He sent to be man's Redeemer. Only a few hours before Jesus addressed the Father, He had said to His disciples, "I am the way, the truth, and the life: no man cometh unto the Father, but by me" (14:6).

To Nicodemus, the Jerusalem Rabbi, He said, "For God so loved the world, that he gave his only begotten Son, that whosoever believeth in him should not perish, but have everlasting life" (3:16). To Martha, sister of Lazarus, He said, "I am the resurrection, and the life: he that believeth in me, though he were dead, yet shall he live" (11:25). The Apostle John wrote of Him: "This is the record, that God hath given to us eternal life, and this life is in his Son. He that hath the Son hath

133

life; and he that hath not the Son of God hath not life" (I John 5:11,12).

Ours is the mission of guiding men into a full knowledge of God and into a personal relationship with Him through faith in His Son, Jesus Christ. Only in this way can they receive the gift of eternal life. Multitudes of people in our world do not have this knowledge, for many do not even know *about* the one and only true God. And multitudes have no knowledge whatsoever concerning His Son Jesus Christ, and therefore they have no personal relationship at all with God. Ours is the high and holy mission of bringing this knowledge to them and guiding them into that relationship through which comes eternal life. Ours is a sacred and solemn mission indeed. When Jesus said, "As my Father hath sent me, even so send I you" (John 20:21), he was saying, in effect, "My Father sent Me in order that men might know Him, the only true God, through Me, His Son, whom He sent; and now I send you to tell them about the true God and about Me, His Son, whom He sent in order that men might have eternal life."

The Bible also tells us that Jesus came to bring light to men who are in spiritual darkness. Zacharias, the father of John the Baptist, was filled with the Holy Spirit and prophesied concerning his son, "Thou, child, shalt be called the prophet of the Highest: for thou shalt go before the face of the Lord to prepare his ways; to give knowledge of salvation unto His people by the remission of their sins, through the tender mercy of our God; whereby the dayspring from on high hath visited us, to give light to them that sit in darkness and in the shadow of death" (Luke 1:76-79). The aged

Simeon, taking the infant Jesus in his arms, exclaimed, "A light to lighten the Gentiles, and the glory of thy people Israel" (2:32). During the early part of His public ministry, the prophecy of Isaiah (Isa. 9:2) was quoted with reference to Him, "The people which sat in darkness saw a great light; and to them which sat in the region and shadow of death light is sprung up" (Matt. 4:16). The Apostle John wrote: "In him was life; and the life was the light of men. And the light shineth in the darkness" (John 1:4,5). John also testified of Him, "[He] was the true Light, which lighteth every man that cometh into the world" (v. 9). Concerning Himself Jesus said, "I am the light of the world: he that followeth me shall not walk in darkness, but shall have the light of life" (8:12).

As already stated, Jesus came into a very dark world. The first chapter of Paul's epistle to the Romans points out the darkness of the world as a whole. A very dark picture is painted by the apostle in this passage. In reading the four Gospels, one discovers how dark it was even in the nation of Israel. But into this dark scene the Heavenly Father sent His Son to bring spiritual light.

Believers are sent on the same divine mission of carrying the light of God to the dark areas of earth, where men still sit in spiritual darkness. There is much darkness in many parts of the world—places where the light has not yet been taken. Almost total spiritual darkness still enshrouds hundreds of millions of men and women—people who were born in darkness, who have lived constantly in that darkness, and who every day are dying in darkness and going out into a dark eternity. There are still vast areas of the earth where total heathen darkness reigns and where Satan's kingdom of darkness is supreme.

Even in North America, though long blessed with the light of the gospel and with the Bible, there is still terrible spiritual darkness, and this seems to be growing deeper and more dense. It behooves us as Christians to heed the words of Jesus, who came to bring light to men. We must take the light of Christ, the Son of God, to our neighbors in our own communities and countries as well as to men and women around the world—across the oceans to other lands and continents and to the islands of the sea. In the words of Jesus, we must bear that light "to the uttermost part of the earth."

It is further indicated in the Scriptures that Jesus' divine role as the Redeemer of men meant giving to the victims of sin and its bitter fruits a more abundant life. He said, "I am come that they might have life, and that they might have it more abundantly" (John 10:10). The Williams translation renders this passage, "I have come for people to have life and have it till it overflows." The Amplified Bible further enlarges, "I came that they might have and enjoy life, and have it in abundance—to the full, till it overflows." It was not the intention of God that man should live a life of misery, distress and despair. God intended man to have a full, abundant, radiant life.

Jesus' parable about the Good Samaritan illustrates this well, showing how Satan has attacked the human race and stripped it spiritually, morally, socially and even physically. He is the thief into whose hands humanity has fallen and by whose hands man has been wounded and left "half

136

dead" along the wayside of life. Through sin Satan has stripped humanity of every vestige of the abundant life God intended it to have. But Jesus, like the Good Samaritan, came to this stricken race to restore it to an abundant and healthy life. He came to bind up the wounds the Devil had inflicted—to pour in the oil and wine of His gospel in order to restore man to a healthy, happy, abundant, spiritual and moral life.

Jesus was moved with compassion concerning the miseries of men. He saw them as lost, hungry, sick and bewildered. And just as His Father's heart had been moved in love to send Christ into the world to redeem them, so our Lord's own heart was moved in compassion toward them. Men were His creatures. They were made in the divine image in order that their lives might reflect and glorify God and that they might live in fellowship with Him. But instead of seeing life among men following this pattern, Jesus saw misery, sorrow, pain, distress, despair and degradation. But He declared His mission: "I am come that they might have life, and that they might have it more abundantly."

To the sinful and unhappy woman of Samaria He said, "Whosoever drinketh of the water that I shall give him shall never thirst; but the water that I shall give him shall be in him a well of water springing up into everlasting life" (John 4:14). This is certainly the promise of a satisfied and abundant life!

Many have found this abundant life in Christ. But there are still multitudes who know nothing about it. There are multitudes who still lie "bound in the darksome prison-house of sin, with none to

137

tell them of the Saviour's dying, or of the life He died for them to win" (Thomson).

After His resurrection Jesus said to His disciples, "As my Father hath sent me [to bring men into a more abundant life according to His will], even so send I you" (20:21). This is the mission of missionaries! This is the mission of the Church! This is the Christian's divine commission! As the Father sent Christ to provide men with a more abundant life, so He has sent us to introduce men to that life. And the gospel which He has given us to proclaim accomplishes exactly this in the lives of those who by faith receive Him.

In bringing this chapter to a close, I want to leave just a brief reminder about the third aspect of Jesus' mission in the world. He came to reveal God; He came to redeem man; and He also came to rear His Church. His own words were, "I will build my church" (Matt. 16:18). This statement revealed the divine purpose of His mission; it is also a divine prediction and promise. He is building His Church in this world. He came into the world for this purpose. From this divine purpose and mission He must not—He cannot—be deterred. The mission must be accomplished; the Church must be built.

Having given His life on Calvary's cross to redeem the Church with His own precious blood, He now sends His disciples forth into the world to carry on the mission of rearing that Church. He determined that after He left this world, the task of rearing the Church must be laid upon His disciples. Therefore He said to them, "As my Father hath sent me, even so send I you" (John 20:21). He laid the foundation, and we must rear the sacred Building.

138

How shall the Church be built? Where shall the materials, the "living stones" which constitute it, come from? Revelation 5 indicates that the triumphant Church will be made up of men and women who have been redeemed by Christ's blood "out of every kindred, and tongue, and people, and nation" (v. 9). This presupposes and demands that the gospel must be published among every kindred and tongue and people and nation. And when He said to His disciples, "Even so send I you," this is exactly what He had in mind. They must go throughout the length and breadth of the earth in order to gather the living stones and to erect his spiritual house, the Church.

Acts 15 indicates that shortly after Pentecost, God, through His servants, began to spread the gospel to many nations and to take from them a people for His name. The first great dispensational visit of God to this earth was by means of the Incarnation. Through Christ, the incarnate One, God came to redeem His people. But the next great dispensational visit of God to the world is by means of evangelization. It is sometimes called the "Dispensation of Grace" or the "Dispensation of the Church," but I like to call it the "Dispensation of Evangelization." It is in this dispensation that God is visiting the nations of the world and taking out of them those redeemed souls foreordained in His wisdom and grace to constitute the Church of the living Christ.

Up to the present time God, through His servants, has visited many tribes and nations of the earth and has gathered souls from among them. The Church of Jesus Christ is being built in many parts of the world. All who have come to a saving knowledge of Jesus Christ constitute the true Church of the true and living God. But there are yet many tribes in this world that have not heard. There are yet some peoples that are not represented in the Church of Jesus Christ. To them He now commissions us to go. Are we willing to go? Are we willing to go on His divine mission, even as He was willing to embark on the Father's mission? Are you willing? Are you ready? He is still saying, as He said then, in essence, " 'As my Father hath sent me, so send I you'—to reveal God to men, to point men to salvation, and to build my Church."

Chapter 17

Like Message

When Jesus said, "As the Father hath sent me, even so send I you" (John 20:21), He very obviously meant He was sending His disciples forth "with like message." His words might have been, "As My Father sent Me into this world with a message, so I now send you with the same message into the world." In fact, the Twentieth Century New Testament translates the text thus: "As the Father has sent Me as His Messenger, so I am sending you." The message and the mission are, of course, necessarily bound closely together. Christ's mission involved a message; and His message was embodied in His mission. And so it is with us.

What was Christ's message to men? We who are Christians think we know well the message He brought into the world. And yet, as the Apostle Peter said, we need to "stir up [our] pure minds by way of remembrance" (II Pet. 3:1). What was this message to mankind? And what is our message to the world?

I want to emphasize four distinct things in the message of Jesus to the world. First, let us consider the fact that His message was one of divine love and compassion.

141

Divine Love and Compassion

His message told of the great love and concern of God for lost and sinful men. To some of us who have heard this truth so long and so often, it becomes a thing taken for granted and we lose the sense of the wonder of it. But to take for granted the fact that God loves us is a sad mistake and a tragic spiritual loss. God was not forced to love us. There would have been ample reason for Him to cast us aside in scorn and repulsion in light of the fact that we who were created in His own high and holy image have so utterly corrupted ourselves and blasphemed His name and nature. Because of our sins, He might well have despised us, utterly shunned us, and withdrawn Himself from us. But no, *He loved us.* He loves the world, and this was the constant message Jesus proclaimed to men during His ministry on earth.

People of Jesus' day were, for the most part, not aware of the great love of God for mankind. In fact, Jesus told the religious leaders of His people that they were very strict about tithing, about the giving of alms, and all the matters of the Old Testament law, but that they passed over the justice and the love of God. He indicted them for glossing over the truth of the wondrous love of God, preferring things of far less importance. They lost sight of the greatest things by focusing their attention on lesser things; they had lost sight of the best for the sake of the good. Having lost the consciousness of God's love themselves, they were not teaching and preaching it to men. Yet this is the very message the human heart most needs and craves.

The people of Jesus' time were not really aware of the love of God, and certainly the pagan, Gentile world was not aware of it. Paganism generally has a very sketchy concept of a God who loves men. Rather their concept of deity is of a god of wrath—one of whom they are in constant terror and whom they are constantly trying to appease with their religious rituals and sacrifices. This is still true today of millions of people in heathen lands. They have no true concept of God and are almost devoid of any consciousness of His love for them. The message they need to hear is the message of John 3:16, and they will hear it only if we proclaim it to them as we have been commanded to do.

What is love? How is divine love to be defined or understood? When the Bible affirms that God loves men and that Jesus proclaimed the love of God to men, exactly what does it mean? I think the best definition of divine love is, "divine self-communication." Divine love is the great heart of God reaching out yearningly in communication to His creatures, even though these creatures are sinful. Jesus proclaimed God's love constantly. His emphasis on God's love reached its pinnacle when He said to the Rabbi Nicodemus, "God so loved the world, that he gave his only begotten Son" (John 3:16).

Jesus often illustrated the love of God by the use of parables. In His parable of the barren fig tree, He told how the owner of the vineyard where the tree was planted wanted to cut down the tree because it bore no fruit. But the dresser of the vineyard interceded and pleaded, "Let it

143

alone, . . . till I shall dig about it, and dung it: and if it bear fruit, well: and if not, then after that thou shalt cut it down" (Luke 13:8,9). This, Jesus was illustrating, is the attitude of the heart of God toward spiritually destitute men—an attitude of compassion and patience.

In the 15th chapter of the Gospel of Luke, the parable of the lost sheep and the shepherd coming to seek it and the parable of the lost son—the "Mount Everest" of all the parables—revealed the yearning, longing heart of God toward the children of men who have gone astray. When Jesus talked to men about God, He pointed out the fact that He has the heart of a loving Father toward His own children. He taught that God is a Father to all mankind in a general sense, as was said by the Prophet Malachi: "Have we not all one father? hath not one God created us?" (Mal. 2:10). Jesus also talked about God as His own Father, in a unique sense, saying, "I and my Father are one" (John 10:30), and calling Himself, "The only begotten Son of God" (3:18). But then He emphasized that God is the Father of those who put their personal trust in Him and who are thus given the privilege of being called "the sons of God" (1:12) in a special spiritual sense.

Before His ascension back to the Father, He said to His disciples, "As my Father hath sent me [to proclaim His love], even so [will I now] send . . . you [into all the world to proclaim that love to all men, to tell them that God gave His Son to die for them and that He desires them to be saved]" (20:21).

144

Divine Righteousness

Jesus also proclaimed the holiness and the justice of God. Over and over He said to the hypocritical scribes and Pharisees and priests of His day, "Woe unto you." He warned men of judgment. He pictured God as a judge and warned men about the danger of the damnation of hell. He told them to fear the One who is able to destroy both body and soul in hell rather than those that are simply able to harm or destroy the body. To the hypocritical religious leaders of His day He said, "Ye generation of vipers, how can ye escape the damnation of hell?" (Matt. 23:33). In fact, Jesus talked about hell as no other person ever did. He said more about hell and gave a more horrible picture of hell than any other person in the Scriptures. And this, too, is the message we must proclaim to men. In preaching the love of God to men, we must not let them lose sight of the fact that God is a God of holiness and justice, and that if they will not accept the gift of His love in Jesus Christ, they will surely inherit His judgment.

Repentance and Faith

In the third place, He preached repentance and faith. We read concerning the time when He began His public ministry, "Now after that John was put in prison, Jesus came into Galilee, preaching the gospel of the kingdom of God, and saying, The time is fulfilled, and the kingdom of God is at hand: repent ye, and believe the gospel" (Mark 1:14,15). This was the same message that His forerunner, John, had proclaimed. Jesus had picked up where John was compelled to leave off and continued the same message of faith and belief.

In chapter 13 of the Gospel of Luke we find Jesus saying to the people of His generation, "Except ye repent, ye shall all likewise perish" (v. 5). In His parables of the lost sheep, the lost coin, and the lost son who came back to his father's house, He declared, "There is joy in the presence of the angels of God over one sinner that repenteth" (15:10). Jesus constantly and strongly emphasized the fact that men must repent of their sins and put their trust in the Son of God, who came to save them. He told them that unless they repented, they would perish. On one occasion, when He was being criticized for eating with publicans and sinners, He asserted, "I came not to call the righteous but sinners to repentance" (5:32). That was His message, and He preached it everywhere. He told men they must repent of their sins and turn in faith to God.

His preaching on faith was just as emphatic as His message of repentance. He proclaimed to men that they must repent and believe the gospel, the Good News. That Good News was that He, the Son of God, had been sent by the Father into this world to give His life as a ransom for the sins of the world and to provide salvation for lost mankind. His message was essentially, "Repent and believe."

Therefore, when Jesus said to the disciples, "As my Father hath sent me, even so send I you," He meant that as the Father had sent Him into the world with a message of repentance and faith for men, they were now to go and proclaim that same message to the world. And we read of the early

146

apostles that their message was always exactly that—repentance and faith. They cried out that men must voice their repentance to God and believe on His Son, Jesus Christ. This was the message of Peter from the Day of Pentecost onward (Acts 2:37,38; II Pet. 3:9). It was the lifelong message of the Apostle Paul, who asserted that he kept back nothing that was profitable to the men among whom he labored. He said, "I have shewed you, and have taught you publickly, and from house to house, testifying both to the Jews, and also to the Greeks, repentance toward God, and faith toward our Lord Jesus Christ" (Acts 20:20-21). In this same context he described this kind of preaching as "the gospel of the grace of God" (v. 24).

Forgiveness and Freedom From Sin

Furthermore, Jesus' message was a message of forgiveness of sin and freedom from its power. This certainly is a great climax to all I have thus far pointed out. For example, in the eighth chapter of the Gospel of John we have the story of the woman who was taken in the act of committing adultery. Her accusers brought her to Jesus saying, "Moses in the law commanded us, that such should be stoned: but what sayest thou?" (v. 5). Then comes the beautiful account of the way Jesus dealt with the sinful woman. After all of her accusers had fled, because of conviction of their own sinfulness, Jesus asked, "Where are those thine accusers? hath no man condemned thee?" (v. 10). Then with grace and mercy He said to her, "Neither do I condemn thee" (v. 11). That was forgiveness. That was pardon, full and free. But He did not stop with that. He added, "Go, and sin no more" (v. 11). That was release! That was freedom from the power of sin!

This is what people all over the world long for above everything else. The human heart longs for the assurance of the forgiveness of all of its sins, and the conscience refuses to be quiet until this assurance has been received. But even beyond that, the human heart longs for freedom from the bondage and the power of sin. Sin enslaves men. It binds them. And though human nature loves sin, it is also true that human nature rebels against sin's bondage.

When some men brought to Jesus a man afflicted with palsy, the first thing Jesus said to the man was, "Thy sins be forgiven thee" (Mark 2:5). His declaration of forgiveness created consternation among the people. They said, "Who can forgive sins, but God only?" (v. 7). But in order to prove His divine nature and power to those people, Jesus spoke again to the man: "Arise, and take up thy bed, and go thy way into thine house" (v. 11). The man got up instantly and walked. That was deliverance from the power of sin and from the fruit of sin. Jesus' word of miraculous power, healing the man, brought silence to the lips of His opponents.

In chapter 7 of the Gospel of Luke we have the story of the woman who came into the house in Bethany where Jesus was being entertained and washed his feet with her tears, wiping the tears away with her hair. But she was not a woman of good reputation. And the host said to himself, "This man, if he were a prophet, would have known who and what manner of woman this is that toucheth him, for she is a sinner" (v. 39). But Jesus turned to the woman and said, "Thy sins are forgiven" (v. 48). That was the word of forgiveness; and that was what she was longing for. She was tired of the way of sin. But then Jesus added, "Go in peace" (v. 50). That was deliverance!

One day in Jerusalem, addressing the Jewish leaders, Jesus said, "If the Son therefore shall make you free, ye shall be free indeed" (John 8:36). Now He was saying to His disciples, "As my Father hath sent me, even so send I you" (20:21). We are to go forth and preach forgiveness and freedom from sin to all men everywhere.

Chapter 18

Like Motive

Let us go a step further than we have already gone and emphasize the fact that when the Lord Jesus said, "As my Father hath sent me, even so send I you" (John 20:21), He meant to send us into the world with the same motive that brought Him into the world and inspired Him on His earthly mission. As His divinely appointed emissaries, we are to go forth with the gospel of His grace, impelled by the correct divine motive in our hearts.

Our knowledge of the Bible and of the very nature of God lets us understand that it is motive that primarily counts with God. Man looks on the outward appearance, but God looks at the heart and the motives within it.

The Bible has considerable to say about heart motives. For example, in II Chronicles 25 we read: "Amaziah was twenty and five years old when he began to reign, and he reigned twenty and nine years in Jerusalem. . . . And he did that which was right in the sight of the Lord, but not with a perfect heart" (vv. 1,2). What King Amaziah did was right, but he didn't do it with a right heart.

And God took more note of his attitude than of his activity.

In the New Testament we read about men who also did good works for God but with wrong and unworthy motives. We read about some of whom it was said that they "preach Christ even of envy and strife; and some also of good will: the one preach Christ of contention, not sincerely, supposing to add affliction to my bonds: but the other of love, knowing that I am set for the defence of the gospel" (Phil. 1:15-17). The various ones to whom the Apostle Paul was referring were all preaching the gospel of Jesus Christ, but they did not all have the right motive. Some who had wrong attitudes preached as they were motivated by envy; others were insincere, motivated by strife and contention.

It is possible to preach the gospel of Christ and proclaim the true teachings of the Bible but do it with the motivation of pride and self-aggrandizement. It is even possible for a missionary to go out to a foreign field for the purpose of self-aggrandizement and fame. This is abominable to God. Personal ambition and personal goals are not worthy motives for proclaiming the gospel of Jesus Christ, even on foreign soil or in a heathen land.

The Lord Jesus commissioned His disciples to go forth, impelled by the same motive that had motivated His coming and His ministry. Jesus knew well that His disciples had previously revealed some very unholy and very unworthy motives for following Him. They had their eyes fixed on prominent seats on His right hand or on His left hand when He would establish His earthly kingdom (Mark 10:37). Our carnal natures have such a detestable desire to exalt self! This is the curse of much Christian work and a great blight upon the cause of Christ. It is altogether too common. This causes the Spirit to be grieved and quenched, and it hinders and deters His work. It lessens the impact of the gospel message.

It is this motive of self-ambition and personal glory that causes much heartache in the ranks of God's workers. Many divisions have occurred in Christian work because of this motive. New Christian organizations have sometimes been formed, not out of divine guidance or spiritual conviction but because of personality clashes. These unworthy motives bring much personal disillusionment to the Christian worker and tend to cause barrenness in his ministry. Not only is it a deterrent to God's blessing and the Spirit's operation, it is often also a stumbling block to the unsaved. Impure motives have caused many failures, dropouts and castaways; and many workers have felt themselves disqualified or shelved.

As Jesus sends His disciples out into the world to proclaim His message of salvation to mankind, it is His deep desire that the same motive which impelled Him to come into the world will also move these who go in His name. Therefore, He said, "As my Father hath sent me, even so send I you" (John 20:21).

With what motives did Jesus come, sent as He was by His Father into this world? He was unquestionably motivated by only pure and holy desires; and it was His will that those same desires would motivate His disciples as He thrust them forth. Let us seek to detect some of the motives which moved Jesus in His coming into the world and in His earthly ministry.

First, He was clearly motivated by His love for His Father. He frequently alluded to this. He said, "But that the world may know that I love the Father; and as the Father gave me commandment, even so I do" (John 14:31).

A conniving lawyer on one occasion tested Jesus by asking, "Which is the great commandment in the law?" (Matt. 22:36). Jesus replied, "Thou shalt love the Lord thy God with all thy heart, and with all thy soul, and with all thy mind. This is the first and great commandment" (vv. 37,38). There is no higher, no holier, no purer and no mightier motive than pure, unadulterated love for the Heavenly Father; and Jesus Himself was constantly motivated by such love during His earthly ministry. He testified, "I do always those things that please him" (John 8:29); this was His constant desire and motive. He loved His Heavenly Father and always sought to please Him. To strive to please one you love is as natural as it is for water to run downhill and as unfailing as the law of gravity.

Jesus was not compelled by external pressures of any kind to come into this world to be the Redeemer of men, but He was impelled by His eternal love for His eternal Heavenly Father. Out of a heart full of love and devotion to the Father He said, "Lo, I come to do thy will, O God" (Heb. 10:9).

Love grants no alternatives. There must be implicit obedience and devoted service. Love demands this of every person who embraces it. Love is highly demanding and deeply impelling.

I shall never forget the look on my father's face and the unusual tone of his voice when, in the act of my saying farewell to him on the eve of my departure for Morocco, he asked, "George, do you *have* to go over there? Can't you work for God just as well in our own country?" You see, Father did not understand the inner, inescapable motive and compulsion in my heart. He could look only at what his physical eyes could see.

The burning question which Jesus put to His disciples after His resurrection, especially to Simon Peter who had failed Him so miserably and denied Him, was, "Lovest thou me?" (John 21:15,16,17). It was as though He were saying, "Simon, love is the overriding answer to all of your failures and faults. What you need above everything else is a heart filled with love. No other motive will see you through. No other motive will cause you to render acceptable service to Me." When Simon persisted that he did indeed love the Lord, the Lord's response to him was, "Feed my sheep" (vv. 16,17). This was the equivalent of saying, "Go out to seek and find the lost sheep. Bring them to the Father's fold. Feed them with My Word and nurture them with the truth. Minister to their needs."

When Jesus commissioned His disciples to go into the world as His emissaries and representatives, He said, "As my Father hath sent me, even so send I you" (John 20:21). This actually meant, "As I am motivated by love for Him who sent Me, so send I you. As I have loved Him, so must you love Me in order that you may fulfill My will."

Why is there so little zeal for world evangelization in the church today? Why is there so little spirit of sacrifice for the heathen? Why is there such a widespread and prevalent indifference to the cause of foreign missions? The very obvious answer is that there is a lack of love for the Lord.

The late A. W. Tozer wrote: "The test by which all conduct must finally be judged is motive. Unfortunately the nature of religious activity is such that much of it can be carried on for reasons that are not good, such as jealousy, ambition, vanity and avarice. All such activity is essentially evil and will be counted as such at the judgment. Christians should take time out frequently to search their souls to be sure of their motives. Many a solo is sung to show off, many a sermon is preached as an exhibition of talent, many a church is founded as a slap at some other church. Even missionary activity may be competitive, and soul winning may degenerate into a sort of brush-salesman project to satisfy the flesh. Do not forget, the Pharisees were great missionaries and would compass sea and land to make a convert."

Second, it is obvious that Jesus was motivated by the constant awareness of His Father's love to Him—that is to say, not only His love to the Father but the Father's love to Him. This love moved, inspired and motivated the Son of Man while He was on His earthly mission. He said, "As the Father hath loved me, so have I loved you" (John 15:9). He also said, "I . . . abide in [My Father's] love" (v. 10). In His prayer in John 17 He prayed to the Father, "Thou lovedst me before the foundation of the world" (v. 24). At His baptism the Father spoke from heaven, saying, "Thou art my beloved Son, in whom I am well pleased" (Mark 1:11). On

155

the Mount of Transfiguration the Father said, "This is my beloved Son: hear him" (9:7).

During Jesus' entire time on this earth He had the constant awareness in His soul that His Father greatly loved Him. He was constantly under the banner of the Father's love, and He abode, rested and revelled in that love. He was motivated and inspired by the consciousness of the eternal love of His Heavenly Father. He knew that God would never demand of Him anything that was not right and holy and necessary. The constant consciousness of the Father's love was sufficient motive for His entire earthly mission.

In turn, Jesus said to His disciples, "As the Father hath loved me, so have I loved you" (John 15:9) and, "As my Father hath sent me, even so send I you" (20:21). Just as Jesus was sent into the world motivated by the love of His Father, so He sent His disciples into the world under the banner of His own love and to be carried on undeviatingly by the constant consciousness of that love. Here is motive enough for missions! Here is motive enough for the evangelization of the world. Here is motive enough to make a missionary out of a Christian young man or lady—the boundless love of Jesus Christ to us. The Apostle Paul testified from personal experience, "The love of Christ constraineth us" (II Cor. 5:14). Even if our love for Him should become cold, His love for us remains constant and unwavering.

The Apostle Jude well wrote: "Keep yourselves in the love of God" (Jude 1:21). But what did he mean? Certainly he could not have meant, "Keep God loving you." Divine love is not based on human worthiness or merit. There is nothing we can *do* to make God love us or to keep Him loving us. Obviously, what Jude meant was, "Keep yourselves in the constant consciousness and awareness of divine love."

Third, Jesus was unquestionably motivated by His own love for lost men and a lost world. In his Galatian epistle, the Apostle Paul described Jesus as "the Son of God, who loved me, and gave himself for me" (2:20). He urged the Ephesian Christians, "Walk in love, as Christ also hath loved us" (Eph. 5:2). In the first chapter of the Book of the Revelation, Christ is described as the One who "loved us, and washed us from our sins in his own blood" (v. 5). He Himself said, "Greater love hath no man than this, that a man lay down his life for his friends" (John 15:13).

No person familiar with the gospel to any degree could ever question the infinite love of Jesus Christ for the children of men, particularly to those who have put their trust in Him. Charles H. Gabriel was so enthralled by the Saviour's love that He was constrained to write:

> I stand amazed in the presence
> Of Jesus the Nazarene,
> And wonder how He could love me,
> A sinner condemned, unclean.
>
> How marvelous! How wonderful!
> And my song shall ever be:
> How marvelous! How wonderful
> Is my Saviour's love for me!

With this motive in His own soul, it is not mysterious that Jesus should say to His disciples,

157

"As my Father hath sent me, even so send I you" (John 20:21). The Father found deep satisfaction in sending His Son into the world, because He knew that His Son loved the people of the world just as His own heart eternally loved them. Jesus Christ possessed an eternal love for the children of men. He wanted to save them from their sin, and it was because of this that He was sent into the world to become man's Saviour. And now He was saying, in essence, to His disciples, "I now send you with the love of My Spirit in your heart in order that you, too, might go forth with the kind of deep, compelling love in your heart for a lost world that motivated Me to go to the cross." For us to go forth with any other motive is to fail to truly fulfill our calling and commission.

The Apostle Paul wrote: "Though I speak with the tongues of men and of angels, and have not [love], I am become as sounding brass, or a tinkling cymbal. And though I have the gift of prophecy, and understand all mysteries, and all knowledge; and though I have all faith, so that I could remove mountains, and have not [love], I am nothing. And though I bestow all my goods to feed the poor, and though I give my body to be burned, and have not [love], it profiteth me nothing" (I Cor. 13:1-3). Missionary endeavor, missionary sacrifice, missionary giving and missionary work become a farce when they are motivated by anything other than true love.

Let us remember that it is the ministry of the Holy Spirit to shed God's divine love abroad in our hearts (Rom. 5:5). Therefore, when we sense our lack of this divine love, we must yield ourselves to

158

the Holy Spirit and allow Him to accomplish that divine purpose in us.

Fourth, Jesus was motivated by an acute awareness that none could perform the mission on which He was sent but Himself. He knew there was no other being in all the universe who could become the Redeemer of men and none other who could make atonement for the sins of the world. And it was this awareness that motivated Him. It was this realization that moved Him to say to His disciples, following His resurrection, when He opened their understanding of the Scriptures, "It behoved Christ to suffer, and to rise from the dead the third day" (Luke 24:46). He knew that there was no other person who could fill this role and pay the penalty of sin for lost humanity. Therefore, He understood and said that the Son of Man must suffer. It was a divine necessity and therefore became a divine decree.

In the Garden of Gethsemane Jesus prayed, "and his sweat was as it were great drops of blood falling down to the ground" (Luke 22:44). He prayed, "Father, if it be possible, let this cup pass from me: nevertheless not as I will, but as thou wilt" (Matt. 26:39). He was fully aware in that dark hour that nobody else could drink of that cup but Himself.

It was, in fact, this very awareness that motivated Him when He came into the world, causing Him to say to the Father, "Sacrifice and offering thou wouldest not, but a body hast thou prepared me: in burnt offerings and sacrifices for sin thou hast had no pleasure. Lo, I come . . . to do thy will, O God" (Heb. 10:5-7).

159

When He told His disciples, "As the Father hath sent me, even so send I you" (John 20:21), it was as though He were saying to them, "I came into this world because I knew no one could perform this mission but Myself; in like manner I now send you forth, because no one can perform the mission upon which I send you but you."

Are we gripped by the realization that we are the only ones who can proclaim the gospel of Christ to a lost world? Are we fully conscious of this? Does this awareness seize and haunt us?

God's great plan of salvation ordained that not even Jesus Himself should remain on earth after His resurrection to preach the gospel to the world. His part was to provide atonement for the sins of men. He alone could do that. But it was not His lot to stay and proclaim the message of reconciliation to the world. That is our task and ours alone. We alone can perform this sacred mission.

Even the angels of heaven are not ordained to evangelize the world. They could never be "witnesses" of His saving grace, since they have never experienced that grace in their own lives. They never were lost; consequently they never experienced redeeming grace and power. How then could they bear witness to the power of the gospel?

When Jesus expounded the plan of redemption from the Scriptures to His disciples, He said, "Ye are witnesses of these things" (Luke 24:48), He meant, "You *alone* are witnesses." When He gave His final commission to them, just prior to His ascension into heaven, He said, "Ye shall be witnesses unto me . . . unto the uttermost part of the earth" (Acts 1:8).

We who are Christians, and we alone, can be witnesses of the gospel to a world in need of the power of that gospel. Should not this consciousness and awareness grip and motivate us, even as Christ was gripped and motivated by the fact that He alone could perform the mission He was sent on by the Father? Did you ever stop to think that of all the creatures in God's great universe, we alone—redeemed sinners, born-again people—can carry the message of Christ's saving grace to those who are still lost and separated from God?

As the Father sent Christ, so has He sent us. None but He could perform the mission on which the Father sent Him, and none but we can perform the mission upon which He has sent us.

Fifth, the Bible also says that the glorious reward and the unspeakable joy set before Jesus Christ motivated Him in His redemptive ministry. Concerning Him the Scripture says, "Who for the joy that was set before him endured the cross, despising the shame, and is set down at the right hand of the throne of God" (Heb. 12:2). "The joy that was set before Him" means the Father's own joy and delight with His Son for completing the mission of redemption. While Jesus was in this world, the Father said He was "well pleased" with His Son. As the Saviour looked beyond the cross, He anticipated hearing also from His Father the words, "Well done!" In John 17 we read how He prayed, "I have finished the work which thou gavest me to do. And now, O Father, glorify thou me with thine own self with the glory which I had with thee before the world was" (vv. 4,5). On the

161

cross He said, "It is finished" (19:30) and "Into thy hands I commend my spirit" (Luke 23:46).

The joy He anticipated was also the joy of the angels of heaven. As a result of His atoning work on earth, there would be joy in the presence of God over even one sinner that came to Him by faith!

The heavenly host sang at His birth, indicating their joy over His earthly mission (2:13,14). No doubt He knew also that they would sing with joy and delight as they welcomed Him back again into the glory.

Then there was the joy of the redeemed ones which He anticipated. This was the ultimate of His entire earthly mission—the redemption of human souls. During all the sufferings and trials of His incarnation, the agony of Gethsemane and the sufferings of the cross, He must have anticipated the song of the redeemed, recorded in Revelation 5: "Thou art worthy to take the book, and to open the seals thereof: for thou wast slain, and hast redeemed us to God by thy blood out of every kindred, and tongue, and people, and nation; and has made us unto our God kings and priests" (vv. 9,10). It is of great significance to note that this song of redemption is joined by "the voice of many angels round about the throne and the beasts and the elders: and the number of them was ten thousand times ten thousand, and thousands of thousands; Saying with a loud voice, Worthy is the Lamb that was slain to receive power, and riches, and wisdom, and strength, and honour, and glory, and blessing" (v. 11,12). Also note verse 13: "And every creature which is in heaven, and on the earth, and under the earth, and such as are in the sea, and

162

all that are in them, heard I saying, Blessing, and honour, and glory, and power, be unto him that sitteth upon the throne, and unto the Lamb for ever and ever." Jesus anticipated all this during His earthly sojourn and redemptive mission. And He was motivated by the assurance that all of this awaited Him.

As Christians, we, too, should be motivated by the fact that our Lord will one day reward us for our faithfulness to Him and to His commission of evangelization. The Apostle Paul wrote: "I have finished my course. . . . Henceforth there is laid up for me a crown of righteousness, which the Lord, the righteous judge, shall give me at that day: and not to me only, but unto all them also that love His appearing" (II Tim. 4:7,8).

In writing to the Thessalonian Christians Paul said, "What is our hope, or joy, or crown of rejoicing? Are not even ye in the presence of our Lord Jesus Christ at His coming? For ye are our glory and joy" (I Thess. 2:19,20).

Note these verses from Psalm 126: "He that goeth forth and weepeth, bearing precious seed, shall doubtless come again with rejoicing, bringing his sheaves with him" (v. 6). Is this not sufficient to inspire us on our world mission of evangelization? Is this not sufficient motive to give to Christ our life, our souls, our all?

Chapter 19

Like Mantle

This will be our final consideration of the Christian's divine commission—the words of Jesus, "As my Father hath sent me, even so send I you" (John 20:21). Let us consider a familiar story from the Old Testament: "And Elijah took his mantle, and wrapped it together, and smote the waters [of the river Jordan], and they were divided hither and thither, so that they two went over on dry ground. And it came to pass, when they were gone over, that Elijah said unto Elisha, Ask what I shall do for thee, before I be taken away from thee. And Elisha said, I pray thee, let a double portion of thy spirit be upon me. And he said, Thou hast asked a hard thing: nevertheless, if thou see me when I am taken from thee, it shall be so unto thee; but if not, it shall not be so. And it came to pass, as they still went on, and talked, that, behold, there appeared a chariot of fire, and horses of fire, and parted them both asunder; and Elijah went up by a whirlwind into heaven. And Elisha saw it, and he cried, My father, my father, the chariot of Israel, and the horsemen thereof. And he saw him no more: and he took hold of his own clothes, and rent them in two pieces. He took up also the mantle of Elijah that fell from him, and went back, and stood by the bank of Jordan; And he took the mantle of Elijah that fell from him, and smote the waters, and said, Where is the Lord God of Elijah? and when he also had smitten the waters, they parted hither and thither: and Elisha went over" (II Kings 2:8-14).

We come now to what is perhaps the most important message of all—the transfer of the mantle of power.

We read in John 20:22, "And when he had said this, he breathed on them, and saith unto them, Receive ye the Holy Ghost." When Jesus sent His disciples forth, He sent them with power like that with which He Himself had been clothed. The story about Elijah and Elisha and the passing of the mantle worn by the former to the latter beautifully illustrates this. The mantle which Elijah had worn symbolized the power with which God had invested him. With that mantle Elijah struck the water of the Jordan River and the stream divided, opening up so that he and Elisha could walk through on dry ground. Shortly after this miracle, as Elijah was being caught up to heaven, his mantle fell upon his successor Elisha, with the wonderful result that the same power that had characterized the ministry of Elijah then characterized the ministry of his successor. Divine power had been invested by the Lord in that mantle.

The famous religious novel *The Robe* is built on the legend that the robe worn by Jesus on earth was invested with a divine, mystical power and that after His resurrection His followers coveted that robe, or mantle, because they felt that whoever possessed it would have the same supernatural

165

power Jesus had. It may have been Lloyd C. Douglas's familiarity with the story of Elijah and Elisha that gave birth to the idea in his novel.

When Jesus said, "As my Father hath sent me, even so send I you" (John 20:21), He was truly saying, "You shall wear the same mantle of power that I have worn during My ministry on earth among you."

Let us now go back to the story of Elijah and Elisha. Elijah had been a prophet who was mighty in word and deed before God and all the people. He was a mighty man of prayer and a mighty man of power. In these respects he was certainly a fitting type of Jesus Himself. Elijah, for example, had performed many miracles. He had multiplied the widow's meal and oil to provide food for the hungry family during the time of drought; he restored life to a dead child, and on one occasion he called down fire from heaven to consume the water-sodden sacrifice on the altar he built to the Lord in the presence of the worshipers of Baal. His miracles involved the very elements of nature, just as the miracles of Jesus had. He divided the waters of the Jordan, which reminds us of how the waves of the Sea of Galilee obeyed the word of the Lord Jesus.

After a long period of ministry, the time came in the special plan of God for Elijah to leave the earth and to be translated directly into heaven. This also typified Jesus Christ, who by direct ascension was taken from the midst of His disciples into heaven, and "a cloud received him out of their sight" (Acts 1:9).

During the time of his ministry Elijah had gained a very devoted disciple, who had been

166

following him for several years prior to this time, living and traveling with him and learning the things of God from him. That disciple was Elisha. Elisha had left his father's house, his family and his occupational pursuit, which was farming. He had made a public farewell feast for his friends, and he had joined the Prophet Elijah. For a period of approximately five years he had served a discipleship with that prophet. This was a time of preparation under his master's tutelage for his future work for God. Elisha was very devoted to his master and had been chosen by the Lord to succeed and to carry on the work of the mighty man—to fulfill his sacred mission. In order to do this he had to possess the same power that Elijah had possessed. So when the prophet said to him, "Ask what I shall do for thee, before I be taken away from thee," Elisha said, "I pray thee, let a double portion of thy spirit be upon me" (II Kings 2:9). In other words, he was asking that he might have the same power of the Spirit of God that his master had possessed, only greater ("a double portion"), in order that he might do an even greater work. It has been pointed out that the Scriptures record the performing of exactly twice as many miracles by the Prophet Elisha as by his master, Elijah.

All this fits the story of Jesus and His disciples. Twelve men had followed Jesus for three years; it was a time of preparation and training for their work in the future, after He would be taken from them. Jesus had told them that the Holy Spirit would come upon them, that He would clothe them with the same power He Himself had, and that "greater works" than He had done would be

167

done by them (John 14:12). Jesus was specifically clothed with the power of the Holy Spirit for His earthly, redemptive ministry. That special robe of power came upon Him in a unique way at His baptism, at which time He was clothed with a specific, divine unction for His mission on earth.

That same mantle of power with which he had been clothed fell upon His disciples when He ascended into heaven. Just as the mantle of Elijah fell upon his successor, Elisha, when Elijah was caught up into heaven, the mantle of the Holy Spirit's power fell upon the early Church when Jesus ascended into heaven.

In chapter 24 of the Gospel of Luke, it is interesting to note the language which Jesus used as He promised and predicted the power which His disciples would receive. His words were, "Behold, I send the promise of my Father upon you: but tarry ye in the city of Jerusalem, until ye be endued with power from on high" (v. 49). In Greek, the original language of the New Testament, the word "endued" meant "clothed" or "robed." He instructed them to wait in Jerusalem until they were "clothed" or robed" or "mantled" with power from on high! Almost every other version of the Bible in the English language except the King James Version translates it, "until you be clothed with power from on high."

This is especially vivid to me because in the Arabic language, in which I preached the gospel for several years in North Africa, this is exactly the way it is translated, "be clothed, or dressed with power from on high." I find it extremely interesting that Jesus should use such a word. He was preparing to send His disciples forth to preach the gospel of repentance and remission of sins in His name among all the nations, and He told them to tarry in Jerusalem until the mantle of the Holy Spirit's power fell upon them—until they were clothed with His divine power.

In the first chapter of the Book of the Acts we find essentially the same thing. Jesus said, "Ye shall receive power, after that the Holy Ghost is come upon you: and ye shall be witnesses unto me both in Jerusalem, and in Judaea, and in Samaria, and unto the uttermost part of the earth" (v. 8). The celebrated commentator Matthew Henry makes this statement: "The promise of the Father in the lips of Jesus is inviolable and the thing promised invaluable." He pictures Jesus saying to His disciples, "Do not go into the world disrobed!" They were not to go into the world spiritually naked. They were not to go out clothed with natural, human power, robed in human ability and in human strength. They were not to thus disgrace His gospel. Rather than letting Satan scandalize them by such nakedness, they were to wait for the mantle of the Holy Spirit to fall upon them.

In the early part of the Book of the Acts we are told how the apostles waited in Jerusalem exactly as He had told them. They tarried for ten full days, until the Day of Pentecost was fully come. And on the Day of Pentecost the mantle of the Holy Spirit's power fell from heaven to earth, and the disciples were clothed with it! Clad with that divine mantle, they went out into the world and proclaimed the message of Jesus Christ, beseeching men everywhere to be reconciled to God. That mantle marked them for life. They wore it through all their days, and wherever they went, they "turned the world upside down" (17:6).

For any of us today to go into the world as representatives of Jesus Christ demands not only that we proclaim the same message He proclaimed but also that we be clothed with the same mantle of power.

There is much confusion today regarding the power of the Holy Spirit. I think this has been a device of the Devil, because he greatly fears that power in any Christian's life. But let me say frankly that there is a mantle of power for every Christian to wear. There is such a mantle fitted especially to each Christian worker and personally tailored to fit all those who go out to the tribes and nations of the earth to be missionaries. The Apostle John reminded his readers that they had an anointing of the Holy Spirit, "an unction from the Holy One" (I John 2:20). We need to claim that unction. We must let the Holy Spirit clothe us. We must let Him cover up our ugly and distracting natural nakedness, our "flesh," and clothe us with spiritual power so that as we go out to proclaim the gospel, the Word will go out "not . . . in word only, but also in power, and in the Holy Ghost, and in much assurance" (I Thess. 1:5).

When Jesus breathed on His disciples and said, "Receive ye the Holy Ghost" (John 20:22), it was clearly a token, or foreshadowing, of Pentecost. It was the counterpart of what He had said in Luke 24: "Tarry ye in the city of Jerusalem, until ye be endued with power from on high" (v. 49). It was what He meant when, just prior to His ascension into heaven, He said, "Ye shall receive power, after that the Holy Ghost is come upon you: and ye shall be witnesses unto me . . . unto the uttermost part of the earth" (Acts 1:8).

They had to have the mantle of the presence and power of the Holy Spirit with them as they launched forth upon this mission of evangelization. They needed this divine power because they were being sent on a sacred and solemn mission. They were to bring to lost, sinful men the news of Christ's provision for the remission of sins.

He said, "Whose soever sins ye remit, they are remitted unto them" (John 20:23). By the preaching of repentance and remission of sins in the power of the Holy Spirit, men would be brought under conviction of their sin and their need; they would, through Jesus Christ, receive the remission of their sins. That was what happened on the Day of Pentecost, when 3000 persons turned to Christ. And it has happened throughout the history of the Church. This is what must happen in the world today. This is what must happen in Muslim lands, in benighted pagan lands, and even in today's "Christianized" world. The gospel must go out, not in word only, but in the true power of the Holy Spirit.

The words spoken by Jesus on this occasion have puzzled many people: "Whose soever sins ye remit, they are remitted unto them; and whose soever sins ye retain, they are retained" (v. 23). It is obvious that only God has the power to remit human sin (Mark 2:7). This power is, of course, shared by His Son, Jesus Christ, whose vicarious sacrifice is the evident basis of divine forgiveness. But, under the power of God's Spirit, Christians may go forth and declare the remission of sins in

171

Christ's name simply because God has already provided such remittance through His Son.

When Jesus said, "Whose soever sins ye remit, they are remitted," He was in effect saying, "Men's sins have already potentially been remitted by My sacrifical death. Therefore, if you go forth and declare to sinners, in My name, that forgiveness is available, they may be assured of full and free salvation. But if you fail to go and do this in the power of My Spirit, you will cause the sins of men to be retained to them." Our responsibility is an awesome one. While the divine power to forgive or penalize a person for sin has never been given to men as a human prerogative, God has placed upon believers the privilege and responsibility of proclaiming forgiveness because He has already effected propitiation and forgiveness through His blood on Calvary's cross.

If we keep the gospel to ourselves and withhold it from the world, the sins of the people will be retained because they have not been told of Christ's provision for them and their need to trust Him. Thus it is that we need the mantle of the Spirit's power and love in order to fill our assigned, awesome mission in the world. The Holy Spirit was sent for this precise mission, just as the Father sent the Son for His precise mission in the divine scheme of redemption.

"As my Father hath sent me, even so send I you" (John 20:21).